CHILD'S PLAY

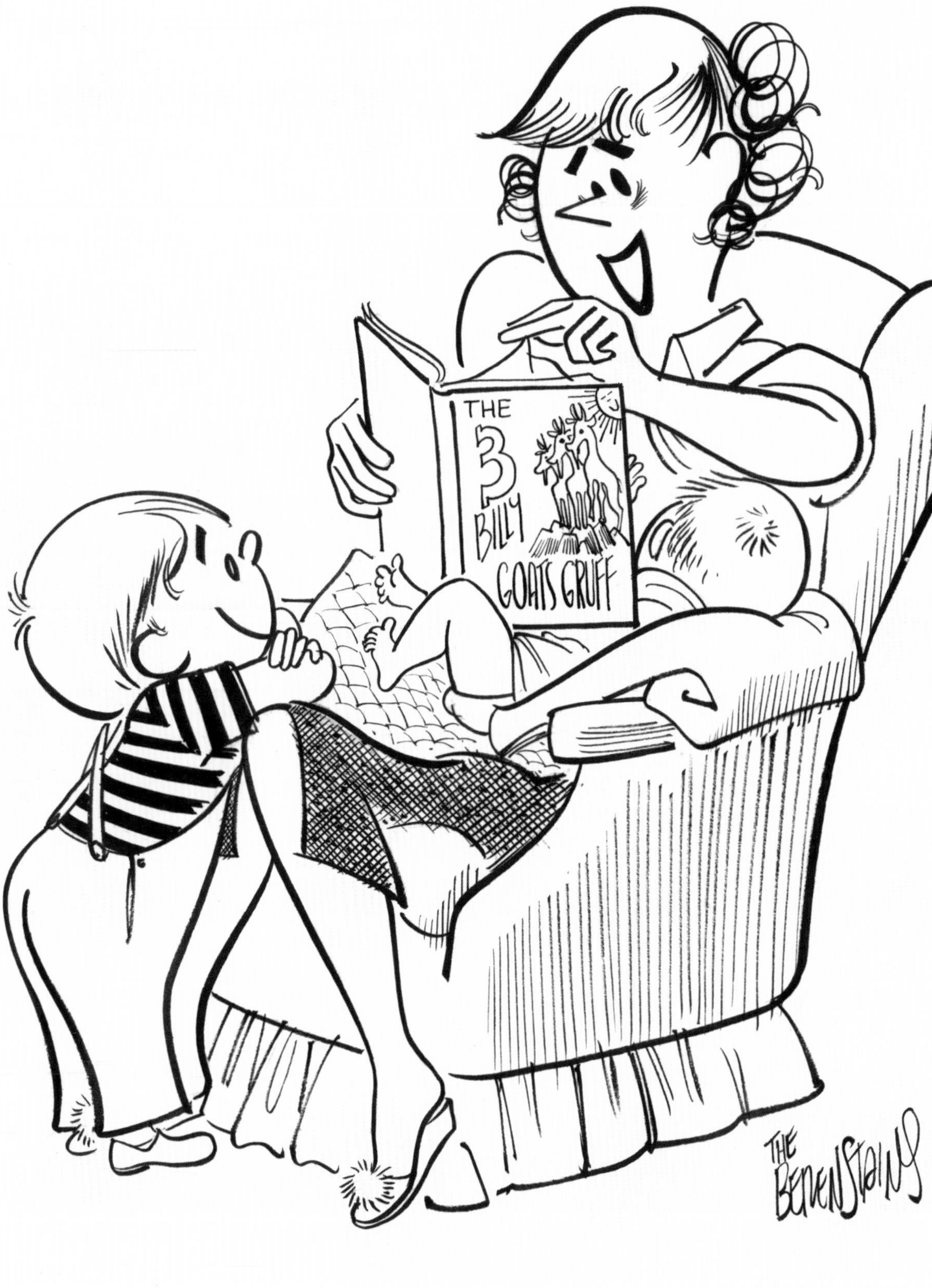
THE 3 BILLY GOATS GRUFF
THE BERENSTAINS

CHILD'S PLAY

The Berenstain Baby Boom, 1946–1964

Cartoon Art of STAN AND JAN BERENSTAIN

By Mike Berenstain

Abrams Inc., New York

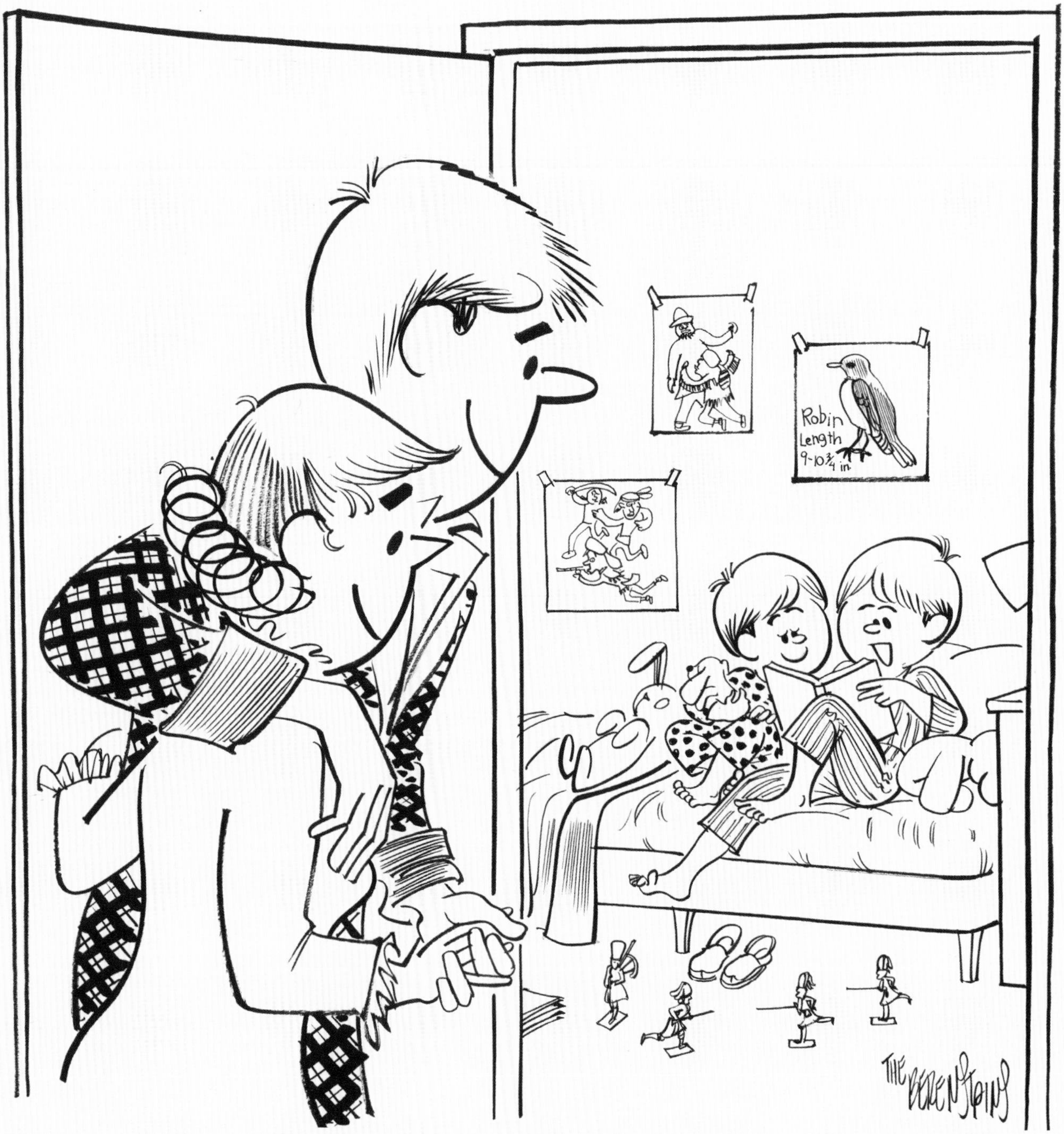
Robin
Length
9-10¾ in
THE BERENSTAINS

In memory of my father

Stan Berenstain
1923–2005

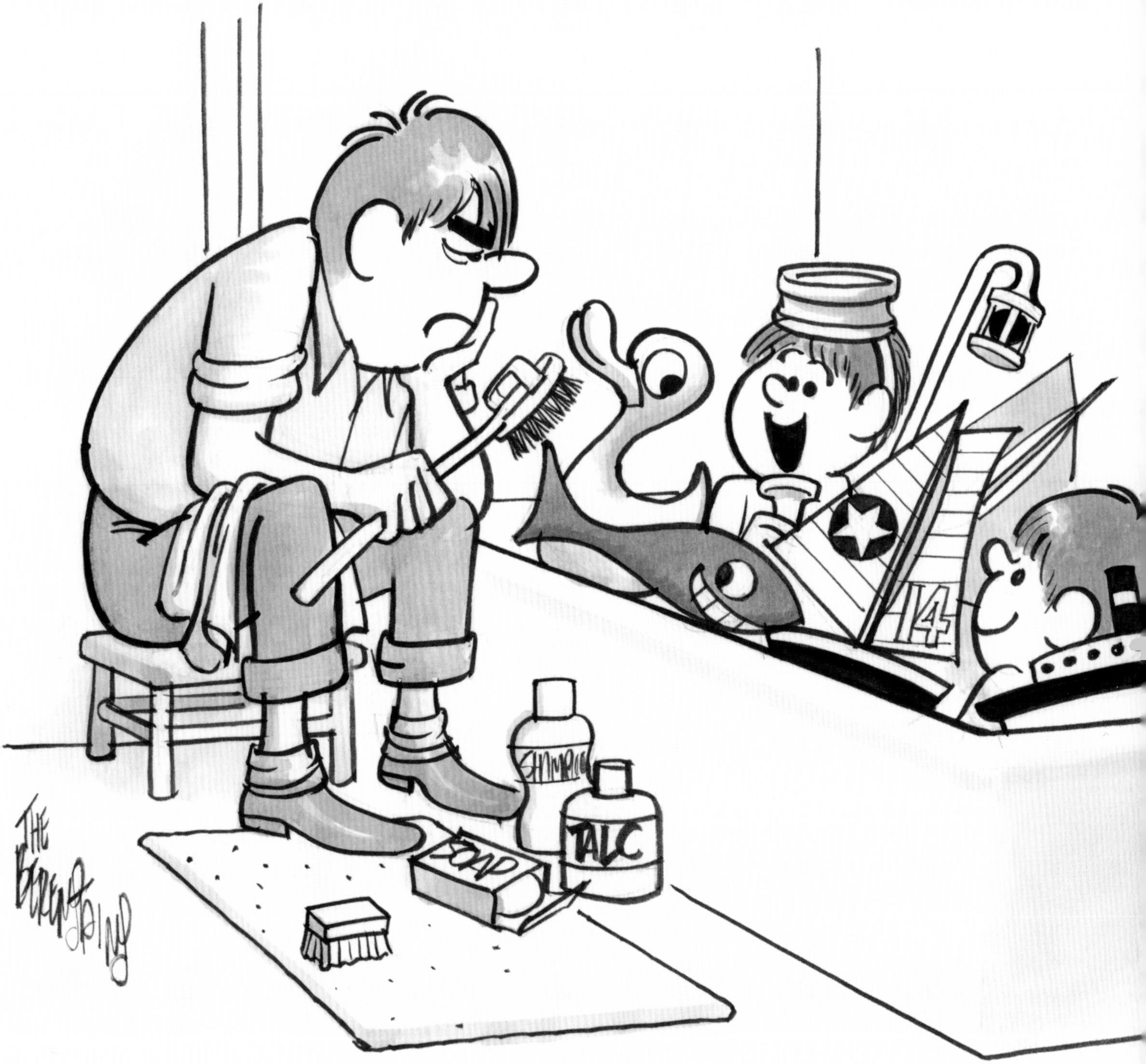
TALC
SOAP
14

BACK THEN

By Jan Berenstain

When asked "What is art?" in the 1970s, cultural theorist Marshall McLuhan replied, "Art is whatever you can get away with." In Stan's and my day, it wasn't. Talented art students in Philadelphia-area schools of the 1930s were singled out by discerning art teachers, mentored, and sent on for advanced instruction by accomplished artists at the city's distinguished art schools. Meeting for the first time at the Philadelphia Museum School of Industrial Art (now the University of the Arts), we both were surprised and bemused that we would meet at all. We came from different high schools—city and suburban. Our backgrounds were different—Jewish and Protestant. But we thought of ourselves as, simply, American and, primarily, as artists.

Comparing notes further, there was something more significant we had in common—our American childhoods. Stan and his sister and I and my brothers had the same toys, played the same games and sports, had the same lessons in school, had similar hobbies, read many of the same books, knew a lot of the same music, listened to the same radio programs and often went to the same movies and museums.

Making model airplanes from strips of balsa wood and tissue paper was a hobby of Stan's. He also recalled sending in box tops to get a Buck Rogers Rocket Gun, which, it turned out, was made of paper. Among his other childhood recollections were stamping tin cans onto his shoes to make a racket while walking down the sidewalk, making a rubber band gun out of strips of inner tube, and sneaking into the back of the horse-drawn ice truck to snitch strips of ice during the long, hot Philadelphia summers.

One of my chief hobbies was making clothes for my two dolls. One doll was an infant with a china head. If I dropped it while playing and it broke, being that it was during the Depression, it didn't get a new one until Christmas. My other doll was a "Mama" doll with enameled arms, legs, face, and head with curled (horse) hair, and a stuffed cloth body with a voice box that said, "Mama!" when bent over. I had crayons and watercolors to draw and paint with, as did Stan, and colored modeling clay that after much modeling of various animals became blended into one color—a grayish brown.

Since my father was an expert carpenter, he was able to build elaborate playthings for us—things we wouldn't otherwise have had in the hard times of the early 1930s. There was a hand-painted, oversize Monopoly board (the reverse side was a checkerboard) and an elaborate pinball game made out of nothing more expensive than plywood and nails.

When, after World War II, Stan and I married and became a cartooning team, we drew on our childhood memories of these toys and games, and of Depression-era back-alley play to create our first cartoons about child's play. When we became parents ourselves, we passed most of our childhood enthusiasms on to our two sons, augmented by many of the new books, toys, and games that appeared in the 1950s. Renditions of these all found their way into our early art and cartoon work for books and magazines, renditions of toddlers Leo and Mike along with them.

This was long before we began to think about creating a family of bears as the subject of a series of children's books. Back then, our people characters were mainstays of the thriving family magazines that, along with movies and radio, were the principal promulgations of popular culture. Magazines like *The Saturday Evening Post* and *Collier's* had a combined weekly circulation of more than ten million and a readership of perhaps fifty million. Along with such monthly magazines as *Ladies' Home Journal*, *Woman's Companion*, *Good Housekeeping* and *McCall's*, family magazine readership was huge.

At the time, the Berenstain contribution to this pre-television world of mass communications was viewed as a contemporary chronicle of the universal experience of American childhood. Today, it can perhaps be best viewed as an opportunity for a nostalgic journey back to the post-war world of Leo and Mike and their fellow Baby Boomers.

CHILD'S PLAY

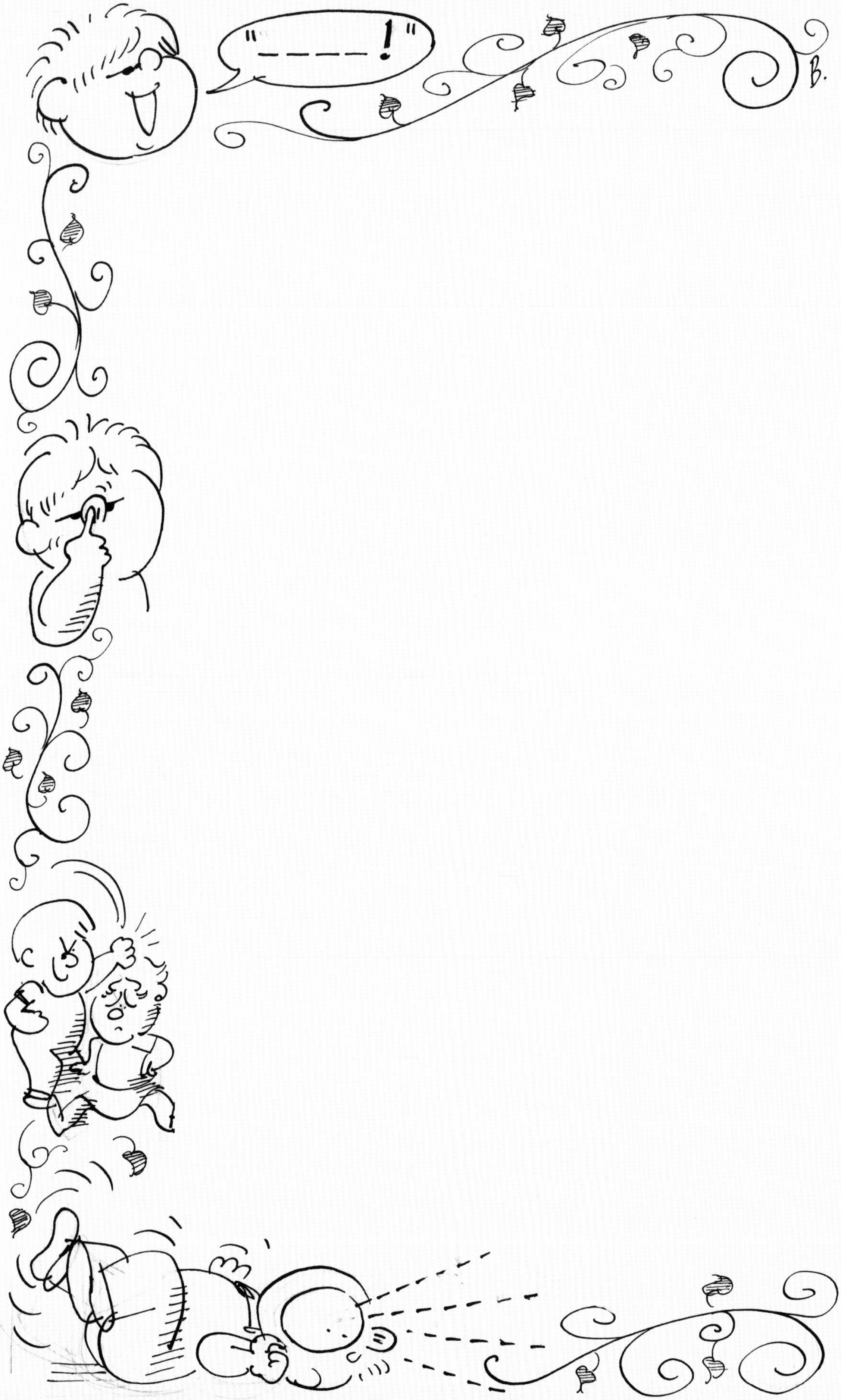
"-----!"
B.

Stanley Berenstain met Janice Grant in Miss Sweeney's drawing class on the first day of art school, 1941. They started off admiring each other's drawings and wound up admiring each other.

They were both born in Philadelphia in 1923 and had even lived in the same neighborhood for a time but had never met. Their mutual art talent led to scholarships to the Philadelphia Museum School of Industrial Art, which finally brought them together in the fateful autumn of 1941. There was time for romance to briefly flourish before the thunderbolt of Pearl Harbor.

He may be ready to try new combinations of food;

FEEDING TIME; *IT'S ALL IN THE FAMILY*; McCALL'S; APRIL 1957

Something of the atmosphere of those art school days was later captured in their *Collier's* magazine cover, *Art Museum*, which depicts a group of art students being harassed by some trademark Berenstain kids. The young man in the plaid shirt conversing with the attractive female art student is a portrait of painter and lifelong friend, Arthur DeCosta. Arthur later painted the official portrait of controversial, ex-cop, Philadelphia mayor, Frank Rizzo. Another portrait appears in the background. The face of Gurney Williams, cartoon editor of *Collier's*, peers out of a Velazquez parody.

ART MUSEUM; COLLIER'S COVER, FEBRUARY 10 ISSUE, 1951

This peaceful, art-filled interlude was disrupted nine months later when Stan was drafted into the Army. He served for most of the war as a medical illustrator in an Army hospital near Indianapolis. Nostalgic references to Stan's army career occasionally showed up in later cartoons—as when a family unearths their dad's old WWII uniform while cleaning out the attic and holds an impromptu parade.

"HUP! Two! Three! Four! . . . HUP! Two! Three! Four! . . . COMPANY-Y-Y-Y—";

ATTIC; *IT'S ALL IN THE FAMILY*; MCCALL'S: FEBRUARY 1964

No trace, however, ever appeared of the gruesome reminders of Stan's real wartime work: his detailed illustrations documenting reconstructive facial surgery on war wounds. He kept them hidden in a bottom drawer away from the sight of his family. The most horrific—of burn victims—we did not find until after his death.

Jan went on with her art school training for a time but eventually left to take part in war work, first doing mechanical drawings of transformers for the Army Corps of Engineers, later as an aircraft riveter working on the center wing section of the Navy's PBY flying boat.

During those wartime years, she got away from the gritty summer heat of pre-air-conditioned Philadelphia by taking a job as a camp counselor in the cool White Mountains of New Hampshire. Her memories of those days looking after a cabin full of homesick and sometimes rambunctious kids were later reprocessed into another classic *Collier's* cover, *Summer Camp*.

Meanwhile, back in the Army, Stan took advantage of his few spare hours to try his hand at the creation of cartoons. Both he and Jan had been fascinated by cartoons as children. Elegantly drawn strips like *Buck Rogers* by Dick Calkins and *Nipper* by the wizard pens-man, Clare Dwiggins, were strong influences on their choice of art careers.

Stan had already experimented with some standard Army fare, drawings of a bumbling soldier named Oglethorpe running afoul of a snafu-ridden military bureaucracy, which had been published in Army newspapers. But he soon grew more ambitious. He saw himself as an artist of some sophistication and so sent a batch of cartoons on literary and artistic themes to a magazine he found in the base library, *The Saturday Review of Literature*.

He was surprised and delighted when he received in reply a check accompanied by a note:

Dear Corporal Berenstain,
Buying all four cartoons. Paying 35 dollars Per. Your stuff is great! Send more!
Yours truly,
Norman Cousins

Figuring that he had discovered a pathway to a life of ease and luxury ($35 per!), Stan followed this advice and began cranking out a series of cartoons about sculptors, painters, and poets.

When the United States government finally decided that it could dispense with his services, Stan was discharged from the Army on April 1, 1946. Having been separated for more than three years, Stan and Jan made up for lost time by getting married twelve days later.

Now that he had stumbled onto the money-making racket of selling cartoons to magazines, Stan enlisted Jan's prodigious art talents in this easy game and they became a cartooning team. They took up residence in a ramshackle, old apartment atop Stan's father's Army and Navy store in a rough-and-tumble neighborhood of southwest Philly. First they simply signed their work, "Berenstain," and sent out cartoons to all the leading magazines.

But they soon discovered, to their considerable dismay, that the only leading magazine that bought any of their offerings was *The Saturday Review of Literature*. Norman Cousins, it seemed, was a big fan, and nobody else. They were able to sell a few spot illustrations to the book review section of the local newspaper and, significantly for their later career, some of these featured images of children reading. But these and other odd jobs could scarcely pay the bills of even their bare-bones, starving-artists lifestyle.

SUMMER CAMP; COLLIER'S COVER, JULY 15, 1950

After months of rejection from such major weeklies as *The Saturday Evening Post* and *Collier's*, Stan decided he was in need of guidance. Boarding the trolley to Center City, Stan headed for the Curtis Building across the street from Independence Hall where he sought a personal interview with the cartoon editor of *The Saturday Evening Post*.

Ushered into this exalted presence, Stan poured forth his saga of unremitting rejection and humbly asked for professional advice in building a career as a magazine cartoonist.

"Berenstain," sighed the weary editor, "let me ask you a question. Do you ever look at our magazine?"

"Of course," replied Stan. "Every cartoon, every week."

"That's surprising. Because every week I get a batch of cartoons from you about stuff like art, music, and history. But *The Saturday Evening Post* isn't about such things. It's a family magazine. It's about getting the last bit of toothpaste out of the tube; it's about ladies' stockings hanging on the shower rail, kids stealing cookies out of the cookie jar, taking the dog to the vet, burnt lamb chops.

Why don't you try doing some cartoons about things like that?"

Stan thought it over.

"OK," he said.

Climbing back onto the trolley, Stan made his way homeward, where he shared his revelation with his young bride and cartooning partner. As a newlywed couple, they had limited first-hand experience as spouses and none as parents. But they certainly had a great deal of experience growing up in families— what's more, in large extended families surrounded by the teeming, child-packed neighborhoods of Depression-era Philadelphia. They knew a lot about kids. Why not, they reasoned, use their own childhood experiences as the basis for cartoons?

Their earliest efforts followed the *Post* editor's advice, closely. They dealt with tried-and-true childhood themes like making mud pies. But their own distinctive creative juices soon began to bubble to the surface. They started to come up with cartoons that conveyed a uniquely childlike perspective on family life.

"No more for me, thanks. I'm full.";
THE SATURDAY EVENING POST; 1947

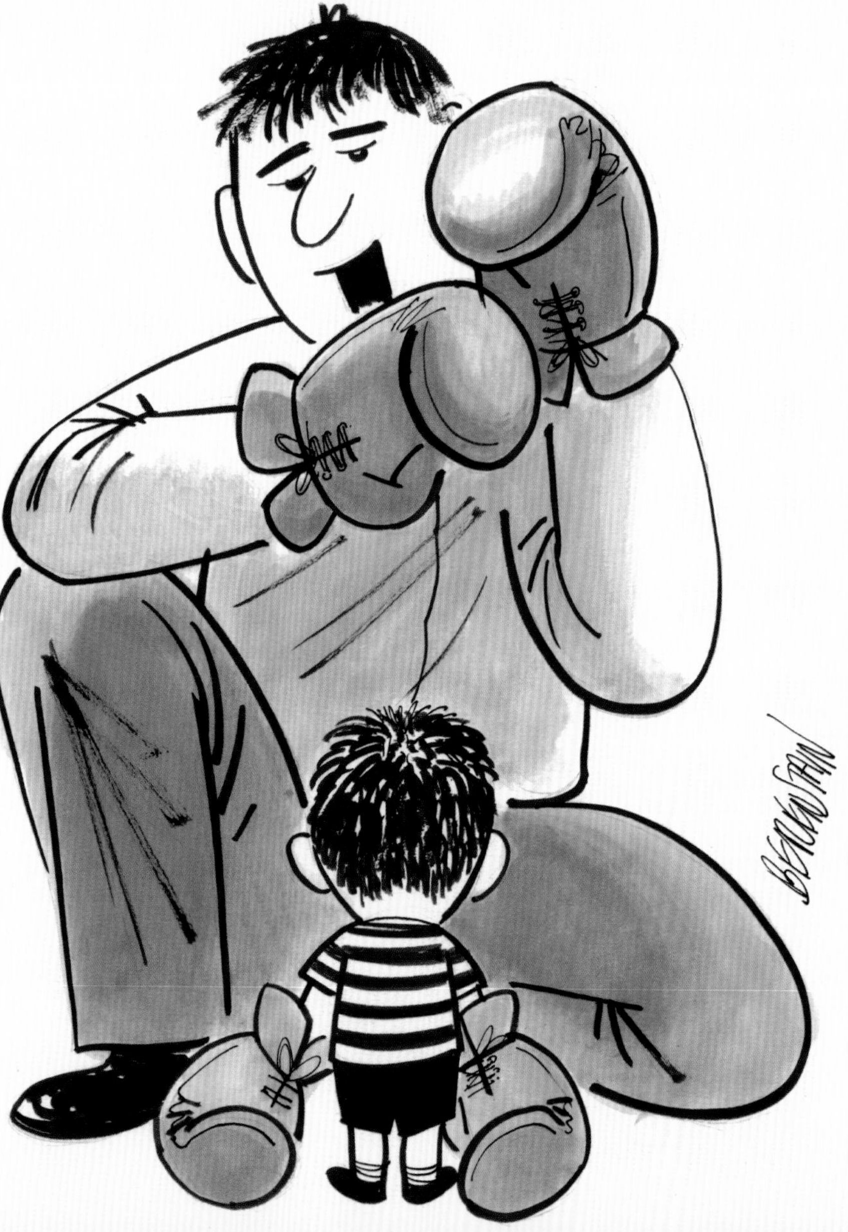
BERENSTAIN

These cartoons struck some kind of a nerve. First the *Post*, then *Collier's*, and then a host of other magazines began snapping them up. Everyone from *The New York Times* to *Successful Farming* were suddenly featuring Stan and Jan's work. When a savvy editor pointed out the fact that being a husband-and-wife team was a good publicity angle, they changed their byline to "The Berenstains" and a historic sixty-year-long partnership devoted to the art of child's play was launched.

Sociologists define the Baby Boom by the steep increase in birthrate which occurred between 1946 and 1964. Although the term "Baby Boom" had not yet been coined, Stan and Jan were in the thick of it, not only as cartoon chroniclers of the generation, but as active participants. They contributed their own first shot to the Boom in early 1948 with the birth of their son, Leo.

They were now cranking out and selling gag cartoons as quickly as they could draw them.

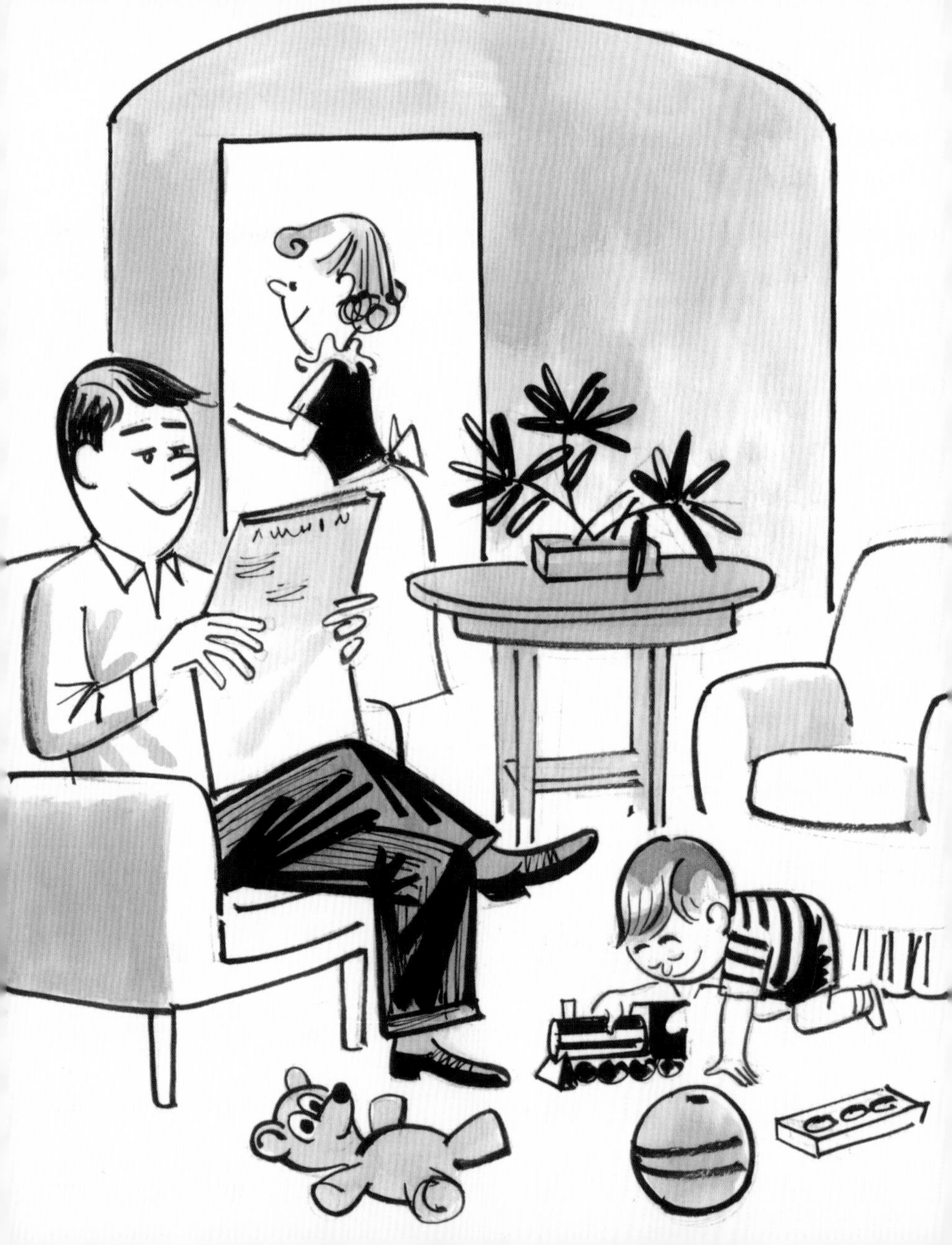

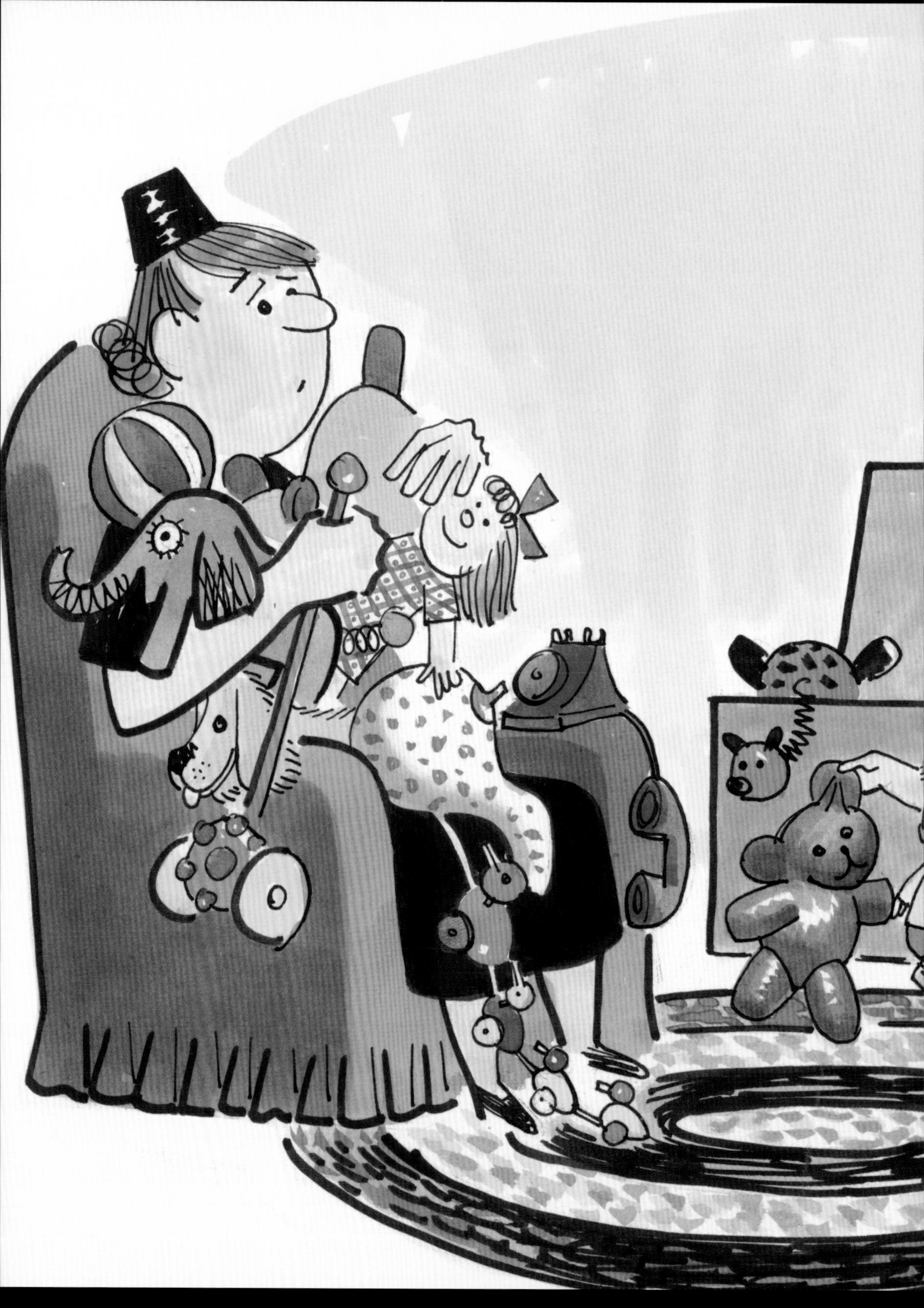

"It isn't often he takes such a shine to a person."; **THE SATURDAY EVENING POST; 1948**

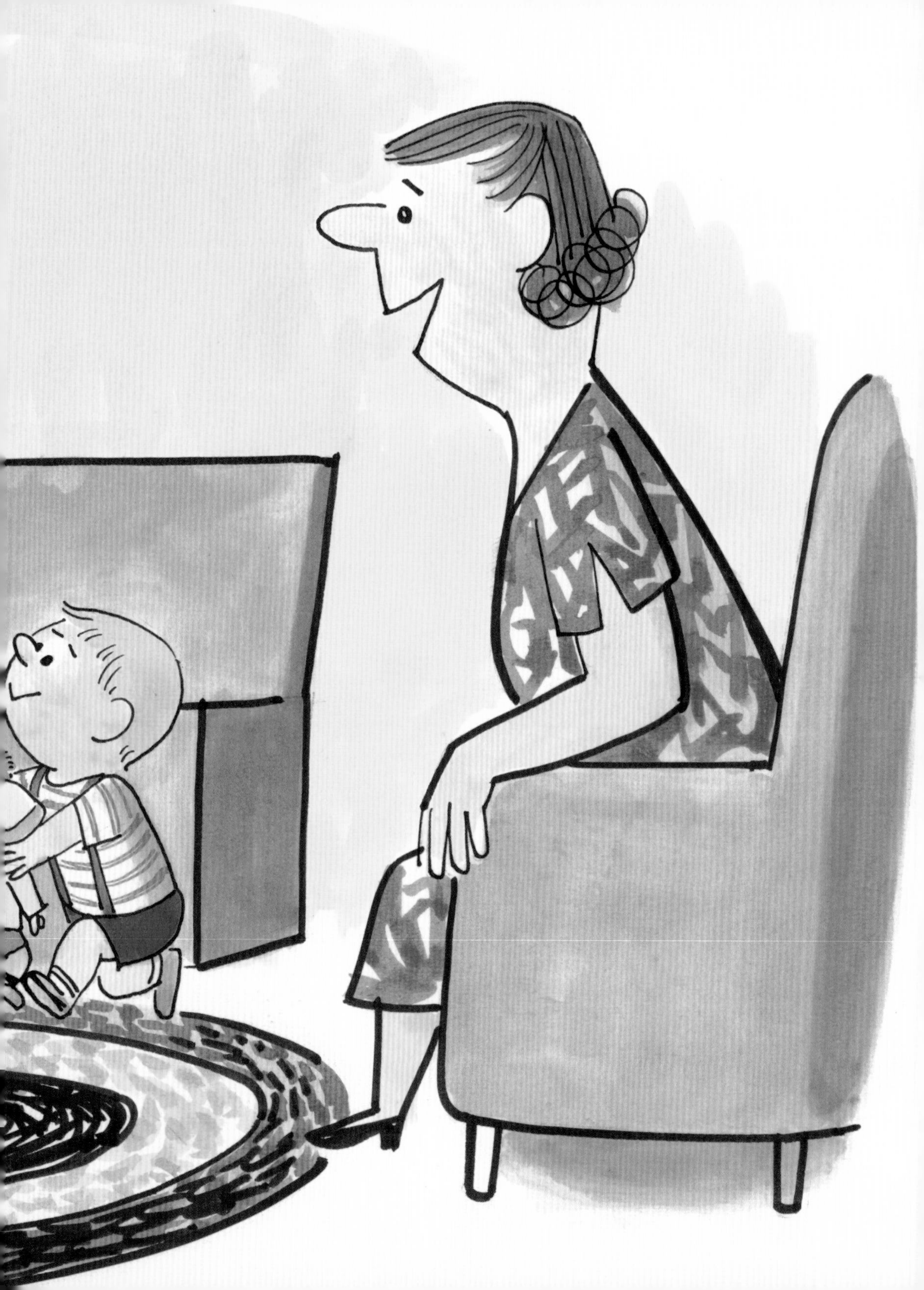

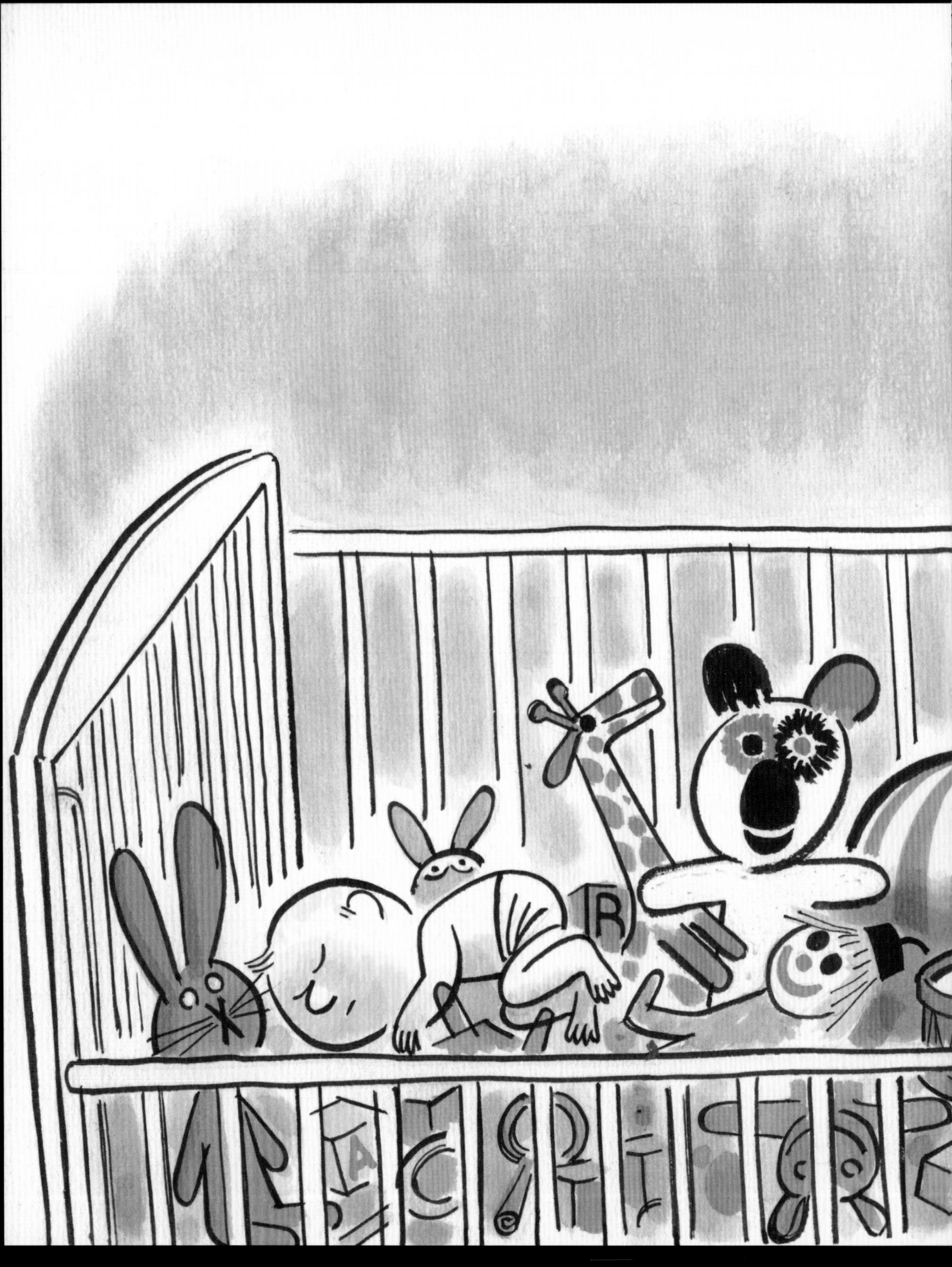

"Oh, I see him now."; **COLLIER'S**; **1948**

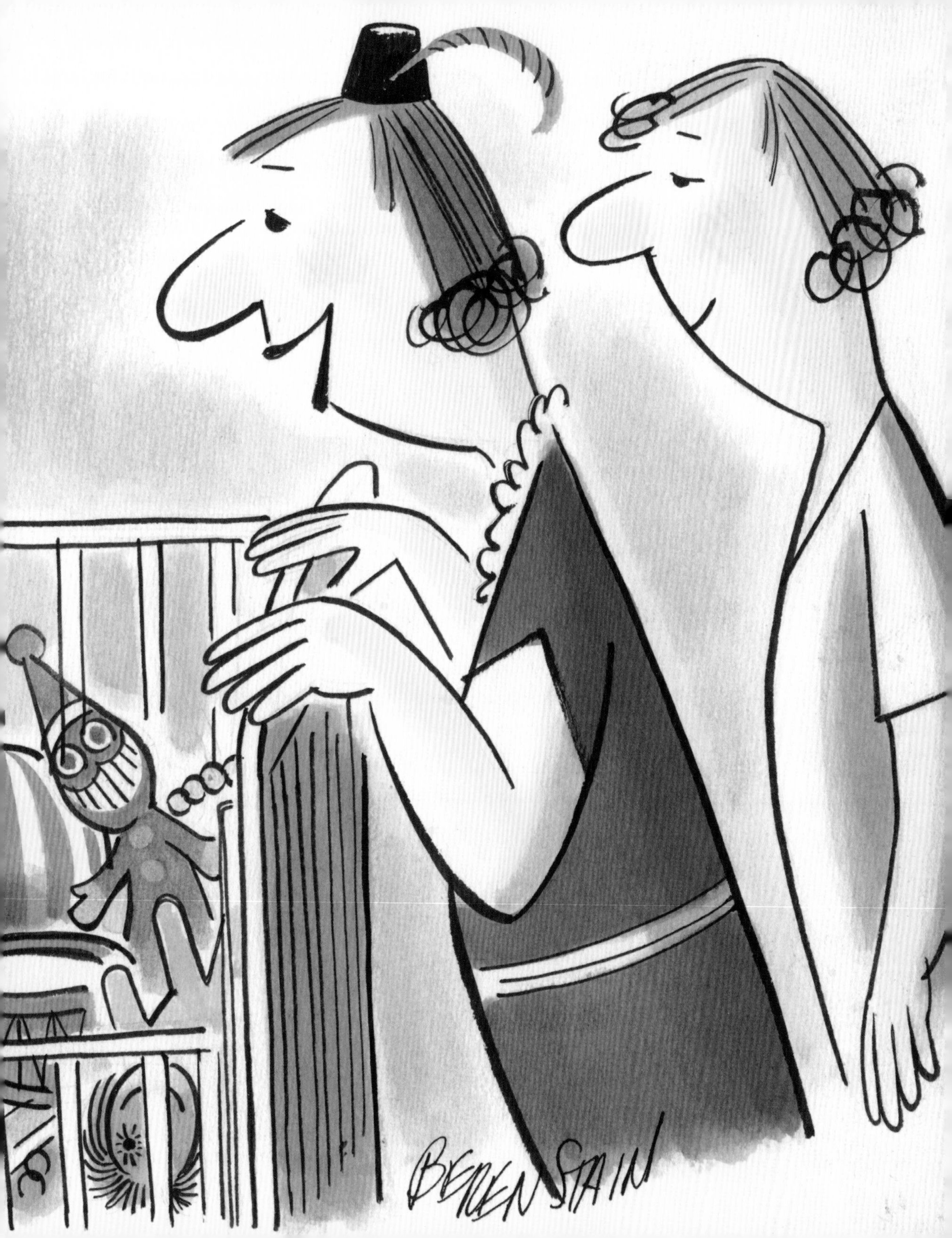
BERENSTAIN

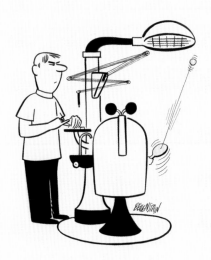

Their standard procedure in those early days was for each of them to sketch a stack of captionless humorous pictures, exchange the stacks, and come up with captions for each other's drawings. The *Post* offered them a "first look" contract—an arrangement whereby all their submissions were sent first to the *Post* for perusal. What the lordly *Post* disdained was then offered to other publications.

There was one fly in the ointment. It was a problem that has bedeviled cartoonists since their art was invented—the tendency of magazines and newspapers to shrink cartoons down to near-postage stamp scale in order to cram more copy, more pictures, and more ads onto a page. The result was that Stan and Jan were forced to make their drawings simpler and more schematic so that they would "read" visually. This was a frustrating restriction for a couple of enthusiastic and ambitious young artists.

They decided to try to break out of this restriction of scale by a radical undertaking: they would create a ginormous whopper of a cartoon which would fill an entire magazine page. To get some notion of the audacity of this proposal, it is well to remember just how huge magazine pages were at that time— ten by thirteen inches was typical. Their target for this mad scheme was their prime customer, the good old *Saturday Evening Post*.

But why should the *Post* want to publish such a gargantuan cartoon, at all? What would it be about? What was the theme? What was the hook? Stan and Jan cast their minds back to their art school days and their studies of old masters at the Philadelphia Museum of Art. They recalled a distinguished predecessor in the art of depicting children at play—Pieter Brueghel, the Flemish master of activity-filled landscapes: harvesters in the fields, hunters in the snow, and children at play. His great painting, *Children's Games*, came vividly to mind—an encyclopedic compendium of all the games played by children in the Low Countries of the sixteenth century. Why not create an updated, cartoon version of this classic vision? Stan and Jan's full-page cartoon, *Recess,* was the result.

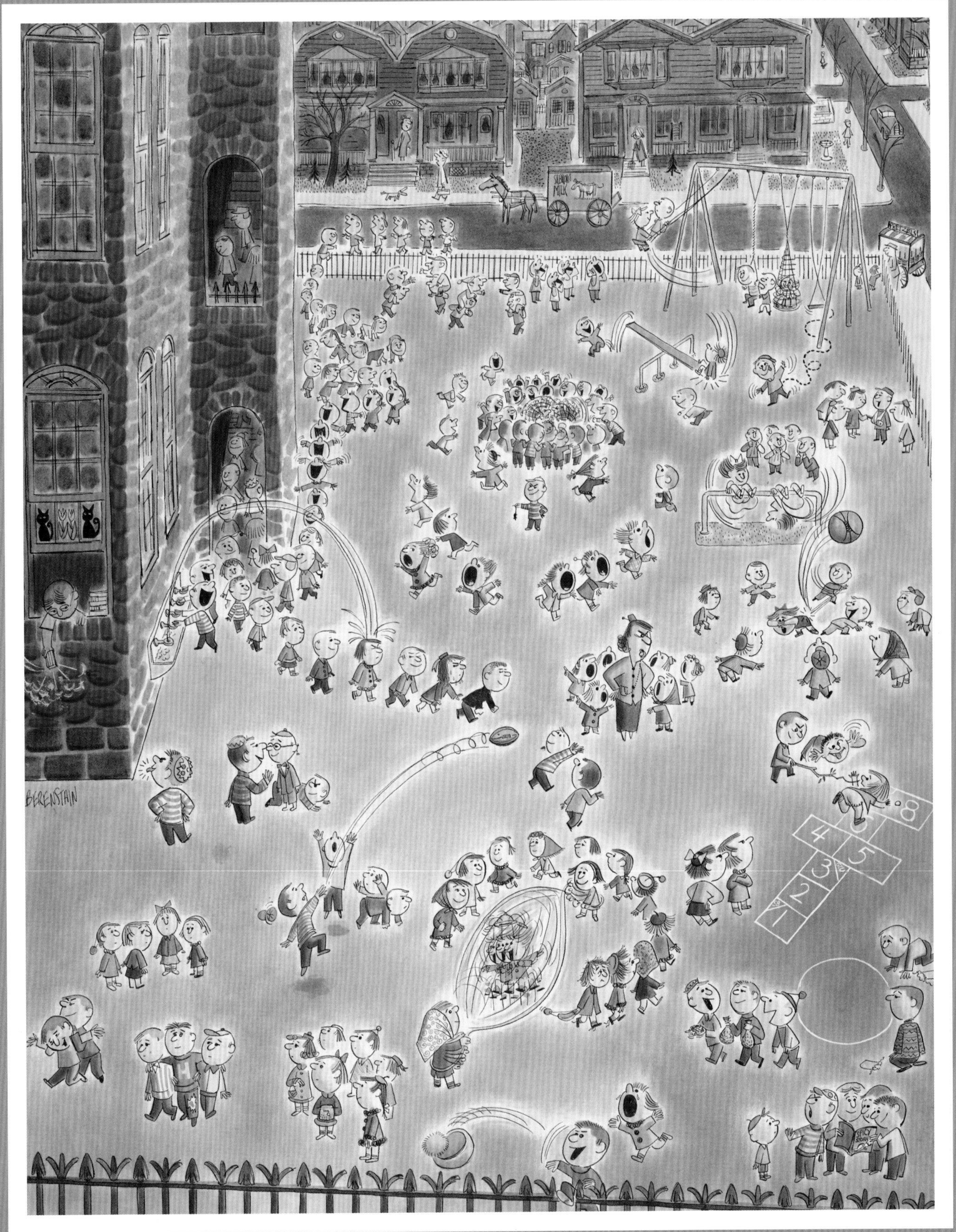
BERENSTAIN

RECESS; *COLLIER'S*; NOVEMBER 6, 1948

This masterful rendition of the playground of a big city elementary school during the throes of that period of hyperactivity known as "recess" contains no fewer than 209 (count 'em—I did) figures, all but eight of them depicting children at play. Included in the turmoil are such standard games as dodgeball, marbles, hopscotch, jump rope, football, follow-the-leader, seesaws, and swings. But a number of less innocent pastimes show up as well, most involving little boys behaving badly to little girls. There are boys looking up girls' dresses, a boy chasing girls with a dead mouse, a boy throwing a girl's hat over the fence and, most disgraceful of all, a group of boys in the corner of the schoolyard taking a peek at a publication with the shocking title, *Spicy Stories.*

Exhausted by this Herculean effort,

Stan and Jan shipped it off to the Curtis Building and sat back to await the accolades which, they were sure, would ensue. But all that ensued was a polite letter of rejection informing them that full-page cartoon features did not fit into the *Post*'s format.

They waited only long enough to recover from their stunned disappointment to submit *Recess* to their second-best customer, *Collier's*. This time, their efforts were rewarded. Gurney Williams, the cartoon editor they were later to depict as a faux Velazquez, loved the piece and bought it for a November 1948 issue. Moreover, he wanted more. He urged them to create a sequel, immediately. This became *Freeze*— a winter version of children at play: skating, hockey, sledding, skiing, snowball fights— you name it, it's in there. It was published in December of 1948.

FREEZE; COLLIER'S; DECEMBER, 1948

Gurney William's editorial judgment was soon confirmed by a flood of appreciative letters from readers. The Berenstains' kids pages were a big hit! He urged Stan and Jan on to even greater efforts. If a full-page cartoon worked; why not a double-page cartoon? The full spread feature, *Gymnasium*, was the result, published in January 1949. Anyone who has ever gone to school and taken "gym" will relate to the semi-tortures inflicted on a flock of hapless schoolchildren in this hilarious scene. The apparatus of ropes, the horse, the rings and mats, the medicine balls, and basketballs are all recorded. The touch of the elevated track circling the interior of the gym places the scene firmly in the aging urban schools of the 1940s.

GYMNASIUM; COLLIER'S, **January 15, 1949**

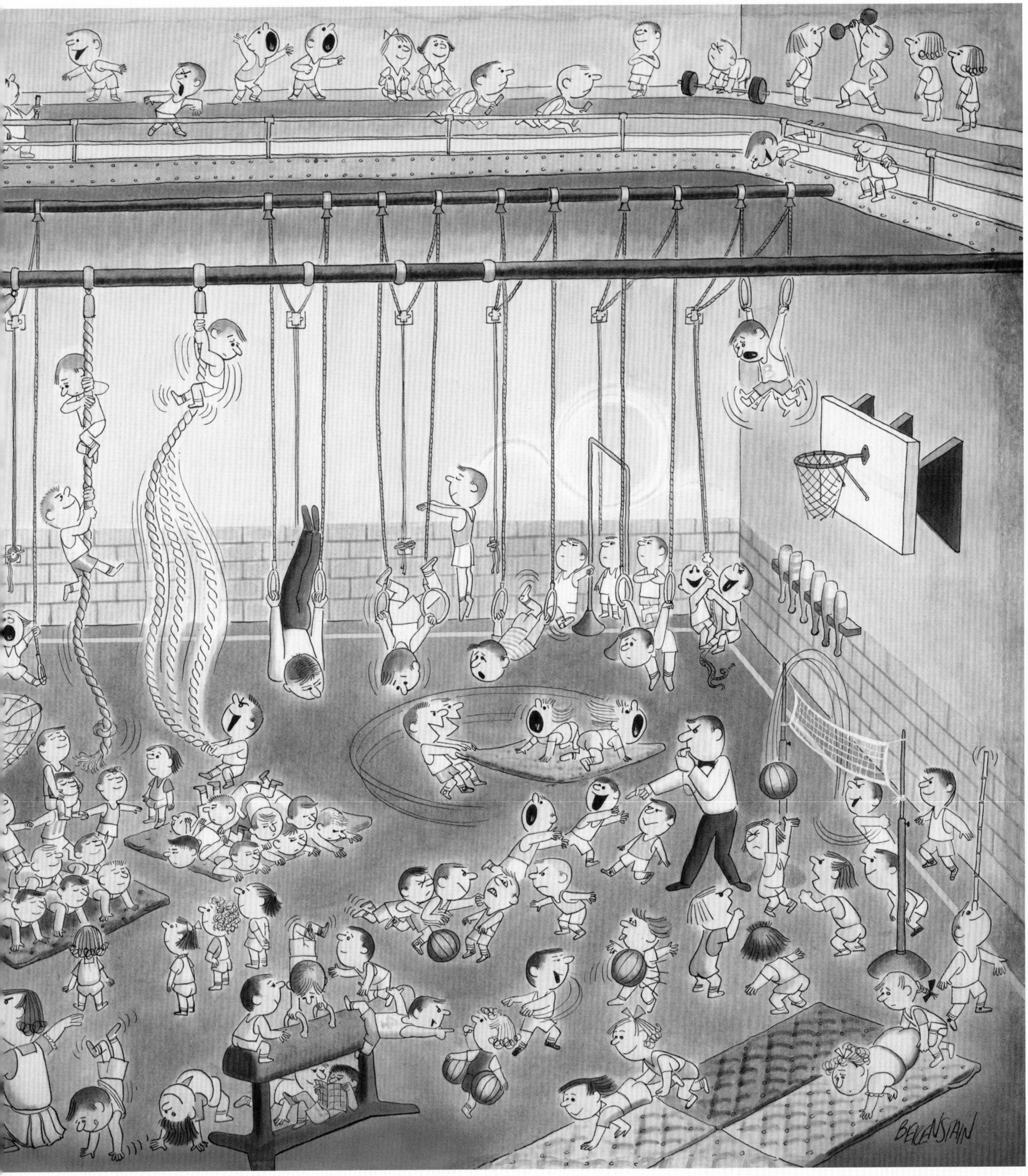
BERENSTAIN

At the same time they were laboring over these massive efforts, Stan and Jan continued to produce a flood of regulation-size gag cartoons chiefly, now, for *Colliers*. They began to focus their efforts on a tomboyish, wise-cracking little girl they thought of, simply, as "Sister"—a cartoon Every Girl everyone could connect with.

People sometimes ask, suspiciously, where the idea of naming the Berenstain Bears by their family roles, "Papa," "Mama," "Brother," and "Sister," came from. They seem to assume it has some subversive ideological import relating to their origin in the turbulent 1960s. But the truth of the matter is that came out of the innocent world of 1940s American family magazines—a world where kids were generically dubbed "Butch" or "Skip" or "Sis"—just another average all-American kid. The humor of the *Sister* cartoons could be sweetly cute and charming. But it could also verge into the slightly edgy and subversive.

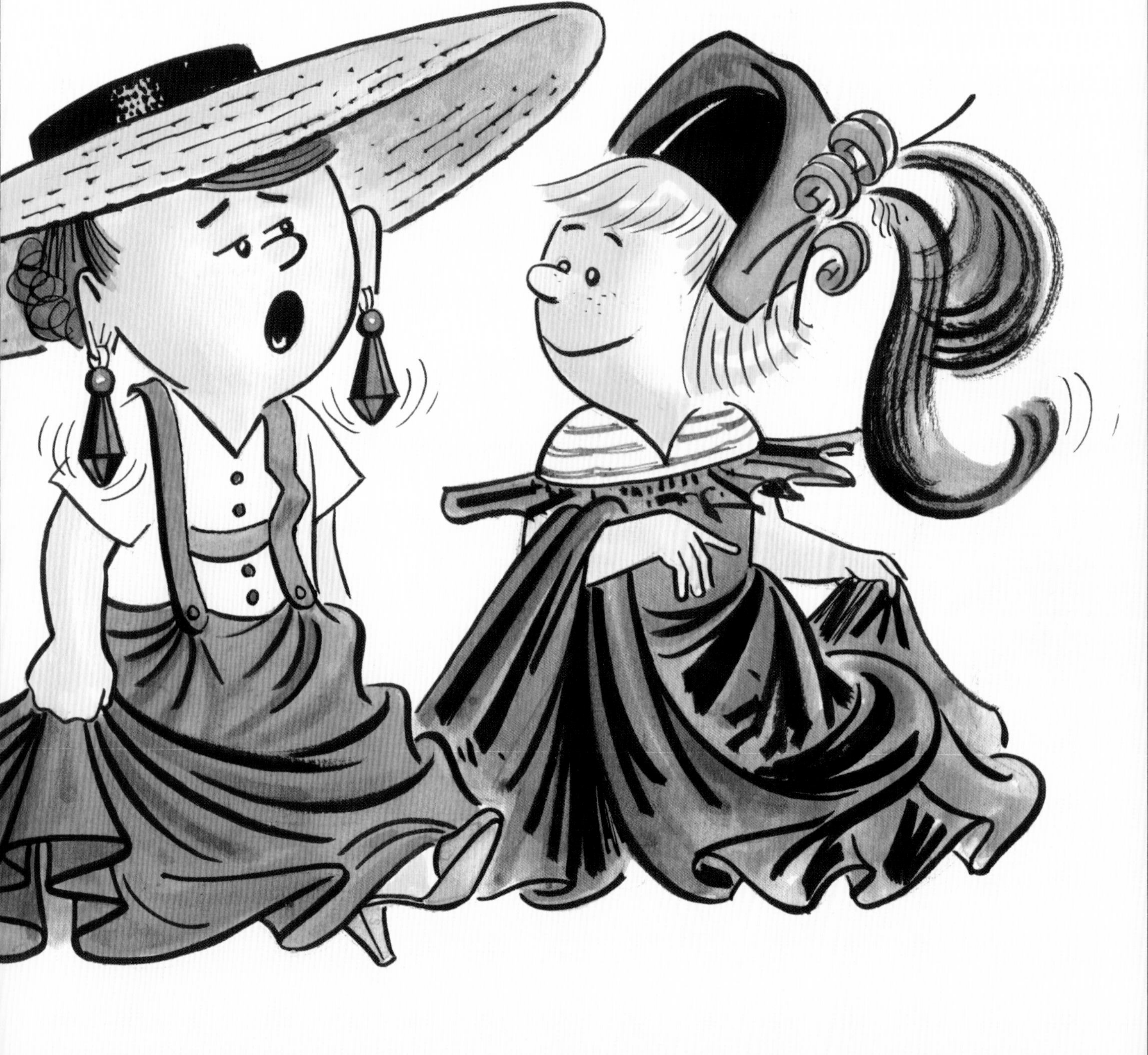

"My ears are killing me!"

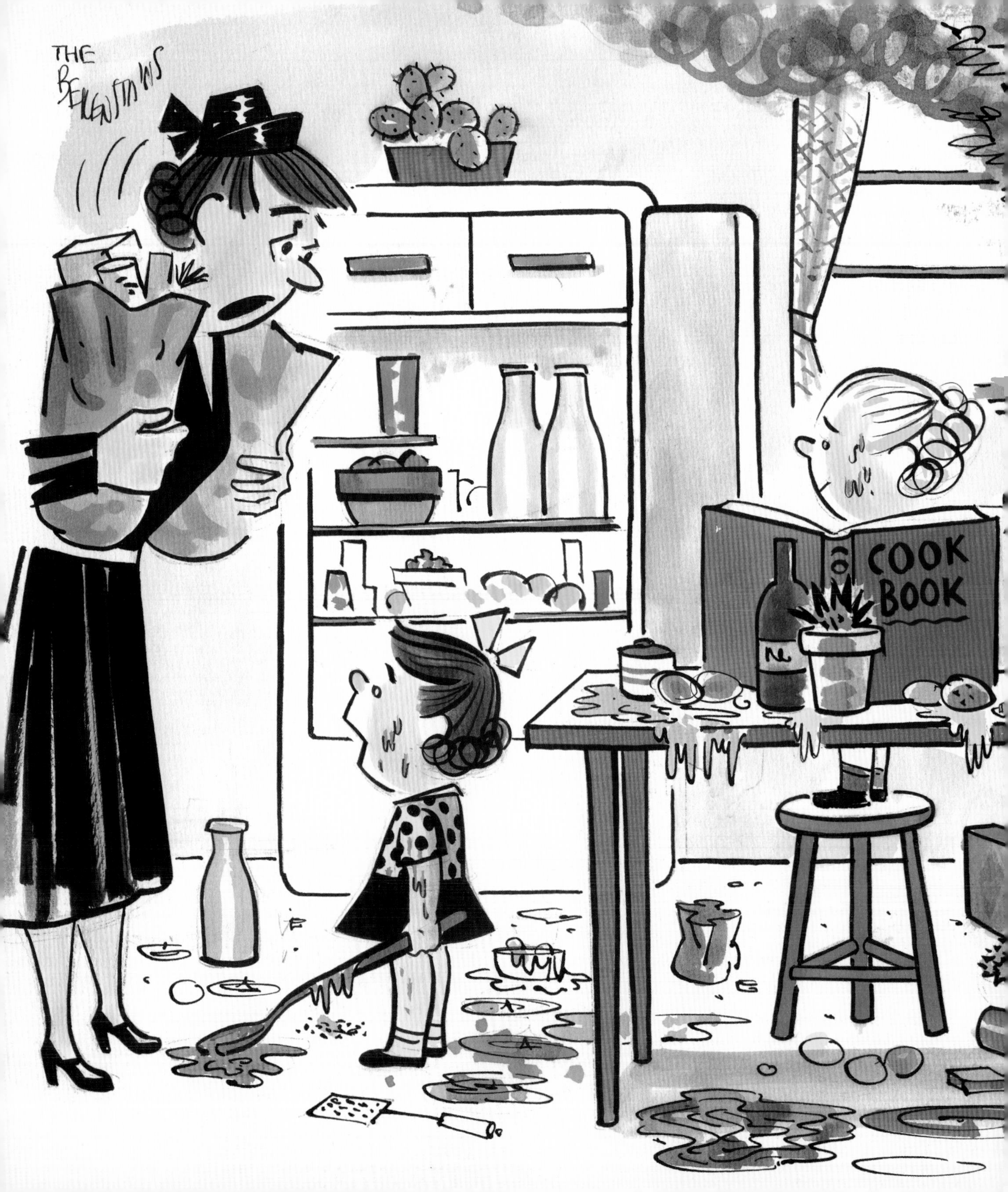
THE BERENSTAINS
COOK BOOK

"We were going to make you something real nice,
but there were too many hard words."

SISTER; COLLIERS; 1949–1952

"That'll never fit Da— . . . , uh-oh!"

SISTER; COLLIER'S; MARCH 22, 1952

"THEY'RE FOR COMPANY? What do you call Peggy, Bill and Lefty?"

SISTER; COLLIER'S; JANUARY 1, 1952

Such was the popularity of their large-format *Collier's* cartoons that it was decided to move them to the magazine's cover. Their first cover feature is perhaps the best-remembered of all. For many it summed up a whole era of popular culture and one that was soon to disappear—the world of that afternoon-long, multilayered entertainment extravaganza, the Saturday matinee. Stan and Jan again produced a crowd scene of tots on the rampage. A few stray adults—an usher here, a bedraggled parent there—try vainly to maintain order. But it is the kids who rule. They drop things off the balcony, they take good aim with pea-shooters and squirt guns, they blow bubbles, climb on seat backs, play the kazoo, drip ice cream and,

in the left foreground, engage in something resembling major combat.

There are a few oases of peace in the theater, as well. One with a personal connection is the little boy in the front row, right, standing on his seat calmly sucking a lollipop while observing the chaos around him. This is a portrait of their son, Leo, who had just turned one.

Over the next two years, Stan and Jan were to produce ten *Collier's* covers and one more interior full-page. They dealt with a wide range of classic childhood scenes and activities: going to the zoo, a birthday party, a trip to the amusement park, a picnic, a football game, a school play, and dancing class.

SATURDAY MATINEE; COLLIER'S COVER, MARCH 12, 1949

THE ZOO; COLLIER'S COVER; APRIL 16, 1949

BIRTHDAY PARTY; COLLIER'S COVER; MAY 21, 1949

AMUSEMENT PARK; COLLIER'S, JULY 23, 1949

PICNIC; COLLIER'S COVER; AUGUST 6, 1949

FOOTBALL GAME; COLLIER'S COVER; OCTOBER 29, 1949

SCHOOL PLAY; COLLIER'S COVER; DECEMBER 17, 1949

DANCE CLASS; COLLIER'S COVER; MARCH 4, 1949

With these prominent creations came a degree of fame and fortune. A *Newsweek* feature of 1949 described them as "a tall tousled young man and his honey-haired wife" and incredulously disclosed that "their drawings last year earned them about $15,000." (Wow!) It also pointed out that their first *Collier's* cover, *Saturday Matinee*, "drew more fan mail than any other cartoon in the magazine's history."

In 1949, $15,000 was not exactly Swiss cheese and it permitted them to follow the great Baby Boom migration to the suburbs. In May of 1950, they decamped their tar-papered, freezing-in-the-winter, roasting-in-the-summer shack of a city apartment for a modern Frank Lloyd Wrightish house on a wooded half acre in tony Elkins Park, Pennsylvania. There they let off the second and final volley of their own personal Baby Boom with my arrival in late 1951.

With the move to the suburbs, too, came a subtle shift in the content of their cartoons. Their earlier work is set in a primarily urban, slightly gritty environment. City schoolyards, narrow back lots, and crowded streets now gave way to wider lawns, broader avenues, and more spacious parks. The school interior depicted in *Kindergarten*, their September 1950 cover for *Collier's*, is the spitting image of Lynnewood Elementary's kindergarten room where big brother Leo and I whiled away a fifties' idyll, building with blocks and playing on rhythm sticks.

My personal favorite among all the *Collier's* art is their final cover feature, *Penny Arcade*. This is a nostalgia-inducing scene from the Atlantic City boardwalk of my childhood: the pre-video game era of mechanical boxers, gumball cranes, skeeball, and nickelodeons.

KINDERGARTEN; COLLIER'S COVER; SEPTEMBER 23, 1950

PENNY ARCADE; COLLIER'S COVER; AUGUST 18, 1951

Stan and Jan's ever-rising professional profile drew the attention of an editor at Macmillan. Since they were so good at creating cartoons about kids, he wondered, why not try their hands at a book on the subject, as well? *Dr. Spock's Baby Book* was, of course, the Bible of child-rearing in the early Fifties and seemed a natural target for a disrespectful spoof. Thus was *Berenstains'* *Baby Book* born, soon to be followed by a sequel, *Baby Makes Four*, and several other childrearing-themed books.

Much of the humor of these books centered on straightforward satire of the "by-the-book" and "he's-just-acting-out" school of parenthood. Stan and Jan were particularly adept at mimicking the pompously professional jargon of the early self-help tomes.

"'. . . Thiamin, Thinness, Three month colic, Throat infections' . . . there it is! 'Thumb sucking!'";
BABY MAKES FOUR; 1957

TOILET TRAINING, Gradually, as Baby grows and gains in confidence he can be introduced to the big toilet and left pretty much to his own devices: AND BEAT HIM WHEN HE SNEEZES: 1969

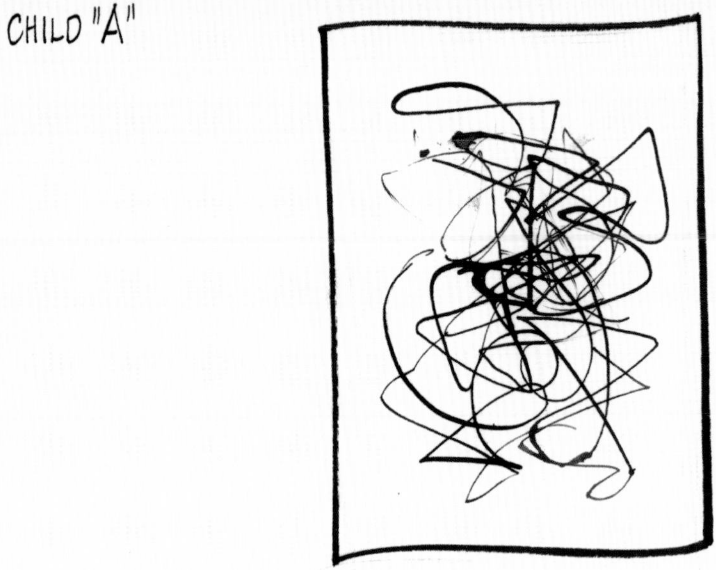
CHILD "A"

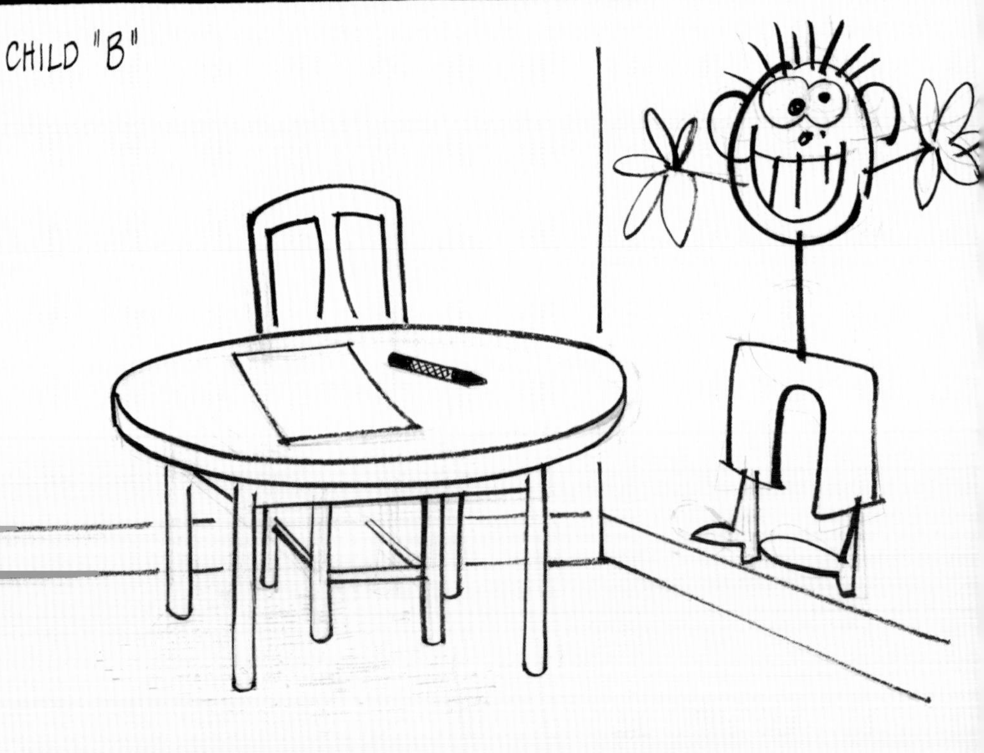
CHILD "B"

ARTICLE OF CLOTHING - 5 %

MATERNAL PARENT - 4.5 %

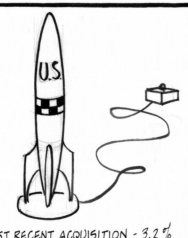
MOST RECENT ACQUISITION - 3.2 %

DADDY'S CAR KEYS - 2.9 %

UNIDENTIFYABLE
NON-FLYING OBJECT - 6 %

MISCELLANEOUS - 1.3 %

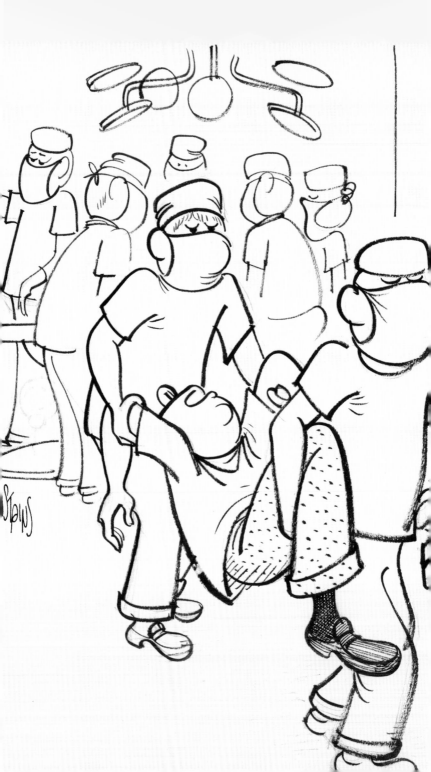

AT NINE MONTHS YOUR CHILD . . . may evidence an irrepressible urge to pull himself up to his feet. **AND BEAT HIM WHEN HE SNEEZES; 1960**

"Now, Eugene, Sally doesn't want to play that game now."

By this time, Stan and Jan had a certain amount of real-life, hands-on experience as parents, and the books actually offered a lot of good, commonsense child-rearing advice along with some acute observations about child development. Still, their primary object was to simply be funny.

With the lavender chalk he starts providing food for the lovely green turkey with feet growing out of his head.; **BERENSTAINS' BABY BOOK; 1951**

You really can't expect your youngster to pick up his far-flung Tinkertoy after being told to do so just once.;

BABY MAKES FOUR; 1957

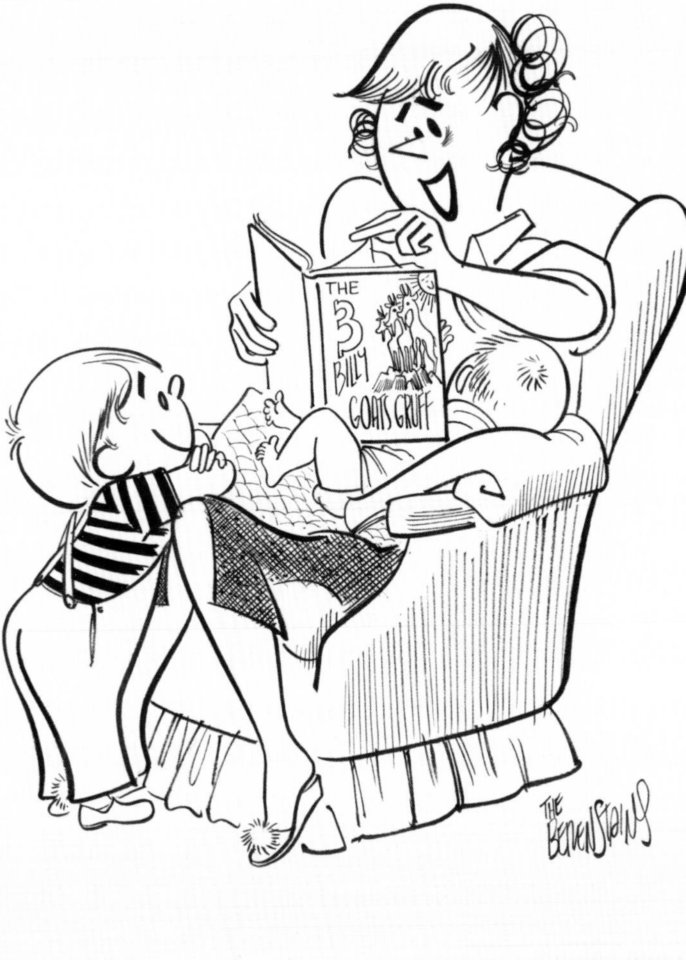
THE
3
BILLY
GOATS GRUFF
THE BERENSTAINS

The mother who tries to play safe by restricting her child to a pencil and bridge pad is just asking for trouble.";

BABY MAKES FOUR; 1957

The difference in size between the largest member and the smallest member of the average kindergarten or first grade is usually pretty astonishing.; **BABY MAKES FOUR; 1957**

"Bang" is as outmoded as "23 skidoo."; BERENSTAINS' BABY BOOK, 1951

He'll be much too busy to notice that the peppermill lamp has been sneaked back onto the drum table."
BABY MAKES FOUR; 1957

During the third year, the problem of Junior's toys begins to assume major proportions.;

BABY MAKES FOUR; 1957

*"'BACK TO THE SEA!!!'"
shouted the brave puppet.;*
BERENSTAINS' BABY BOOK; 1951

Their idea of recess fun is roughly equivalent to an Australian tag-team match without benefit of referee.;
BABY MAKES FOUR; 1957

A good loud bell and an old watch make the job of referee more palatable.; BABY MAKES FOUR; 1957

Pregnancy: It may range in intensity from the tiniest flutter . . . ;

AND BEAT HIM WHEN HE SNEEZES; 1960

AND BEAT HIM WHEN HE SNEEZES: 1960

"Dis is my Meriwe'er Lewis costume," Mike announces for the benefit of anyone who may be interested.; **BABY MAKES FOUR; 1957**

*Never again will you wonder what's
in that old Whitman Sampler box,
and idly lift the lid.;*
BABY MAKES FOUR; 1957

PREGNANCY: . . . certain kinds of cars . . . and sudden starts and stops.; AND BEAT HIM WHEN HE SNEEZES; 1960

It has been sometimes remarked that my parents' marriage must have been extraordinarily close and strong to so successfully survive the stresses of both a professional and personal partnership. This is true, especially considering that, from the day of their wedding to Stan's death in November of 2005, they spent about 99.9 percent of their lives in the same room! I have often thought that the principle reason for their ability to communicate to their audience so effectively on the subject of marriage and family was the intensity of their own commitment to the institution.

He was delighted to sit by and gurgle at the fun . . . ; **BABY MAKES FOUR; 1957**

The rumpled but happy parents were beaming foolishly down on them.; BABY MAKES FOUR; 1957

AT THREE MONTHS YOUR CHILD . . . smiles in response to friendly overtures . . .
is able to locate source of light; AND BEAT HIM WHEN HE SNEEZES; 1960

Berenstain Family Christmas Card, circa 1950

But, in spite of all their success as cartoonists and, now, as authors, a further achievement beckoned to the young cartooning pair. In the early 1950s, the ultimate success story for any cartoonist was the creation of a daily comic strip in a popular newspaper. That was the true big time—the world of *L'il Abner*, *Pogo*, *Beetle Bailey* and the avant-garde newcomer, *Peanuts*. And so, tempted by this tantalizing mirage, the ever-ambitious Stan and Jan embarked on an ill-fated excursion from the fertile valleys of weekly magazines to the harsh and barren uplands of the funny pages.

Sister, the ongoing panel cartoon they had produced for *Collier's*, was the nucleus of the project. It was popular—a book collection was published in 1952—and many of the gags had already taken on a sequential form similar to that of a comic strip. Why not, schemed Stan and Jan, extend this successful magazine cartoon into a daily newspaper comic?

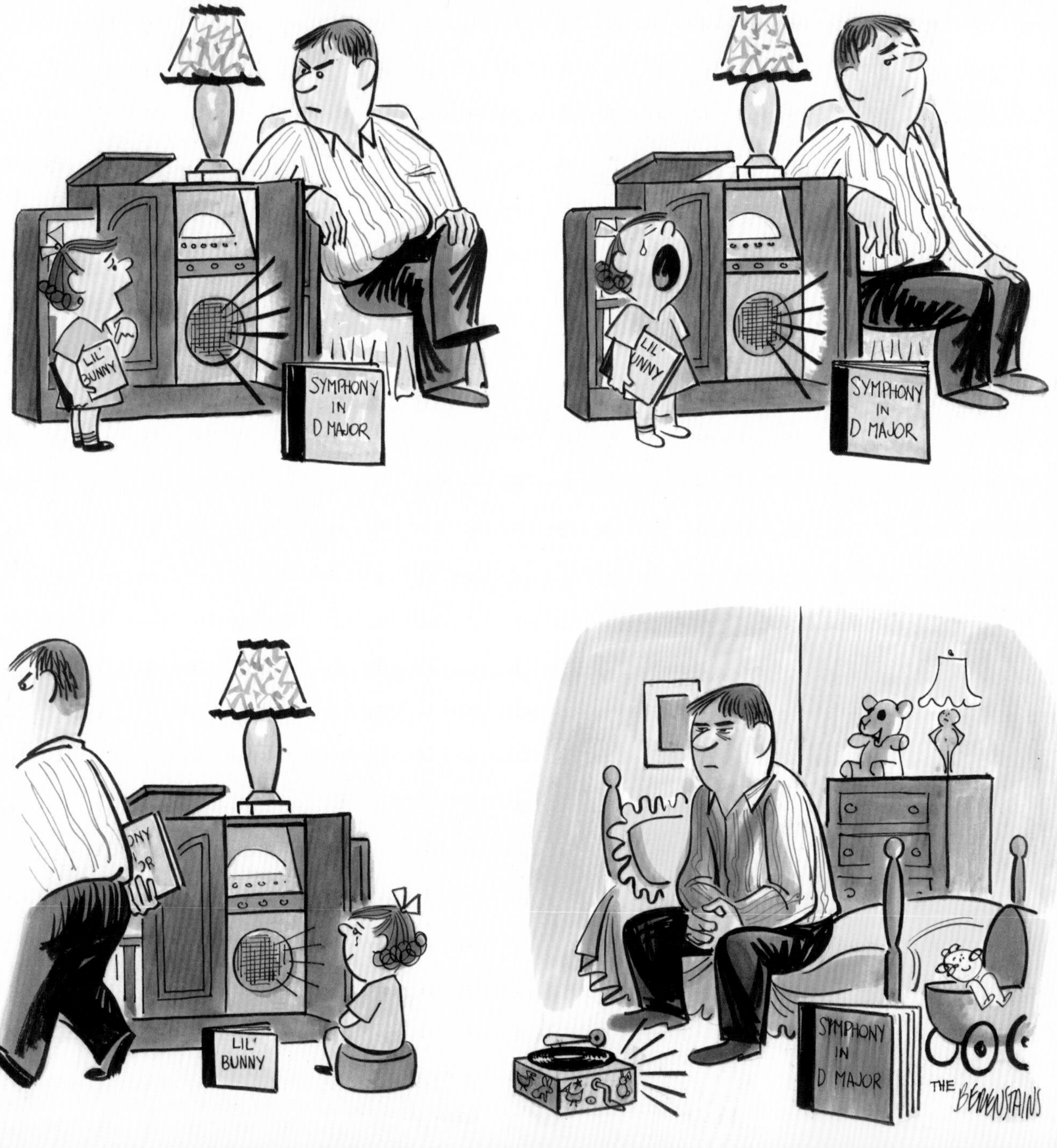
LIL' BUNNY
SYMPHONY IN D MAJOR
LIL' UNNY
SYMPHONY IN D MAJOR
LIL' BUNNY
SYMPHONY IN D MAJOR
THE BERENSTAINS

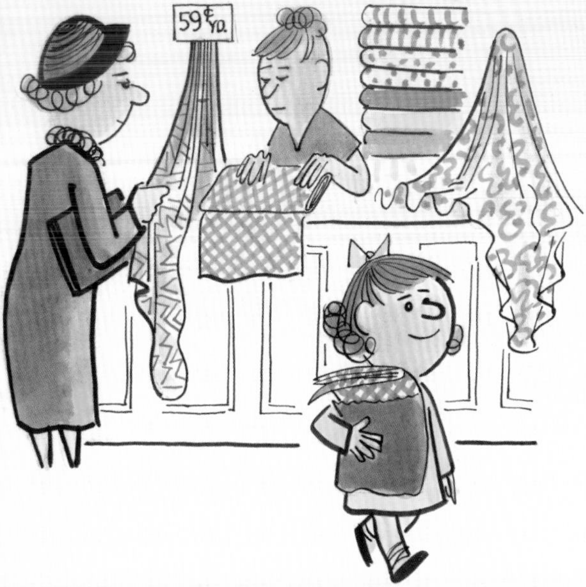
59¢ YD.

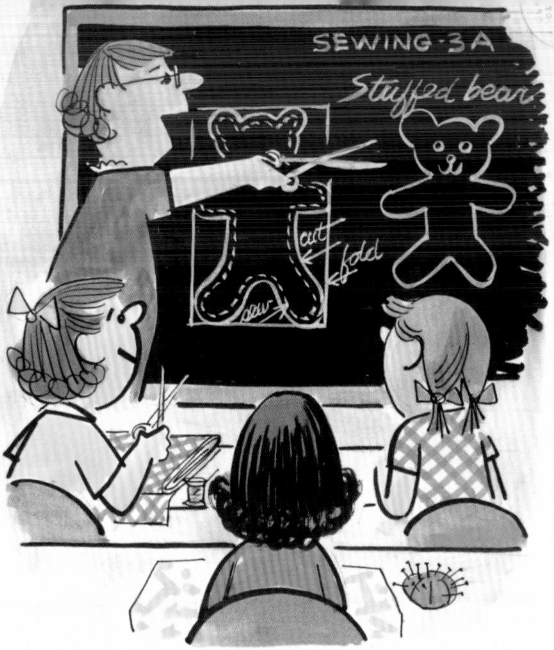
SEWING-3A
Stuffed bear
cut
fold
sew

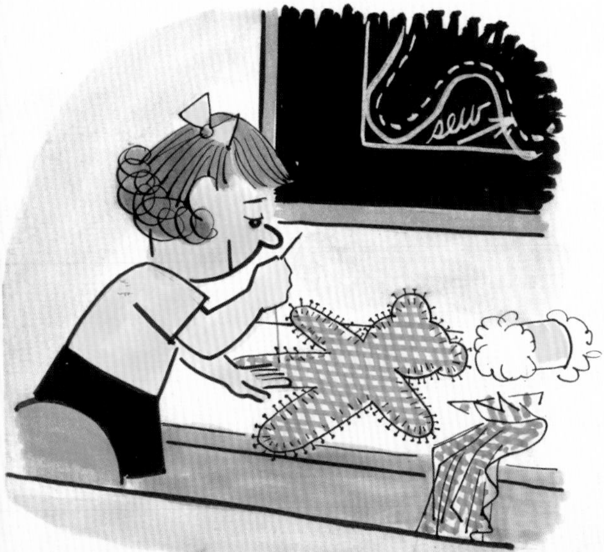
sew

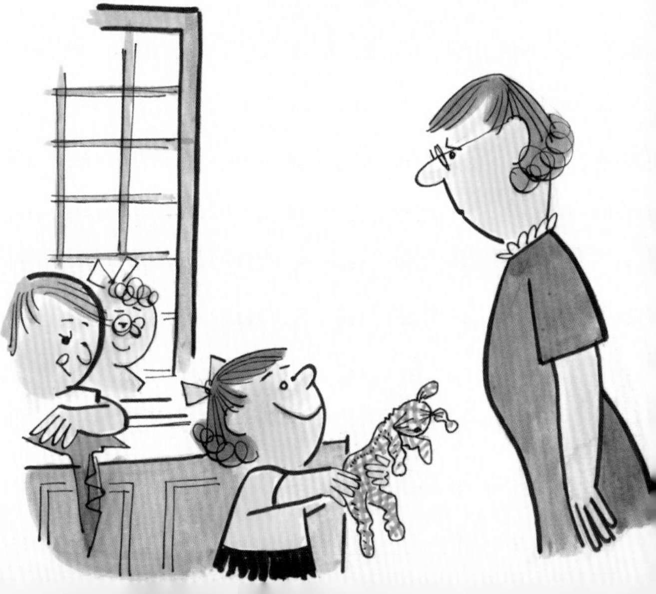

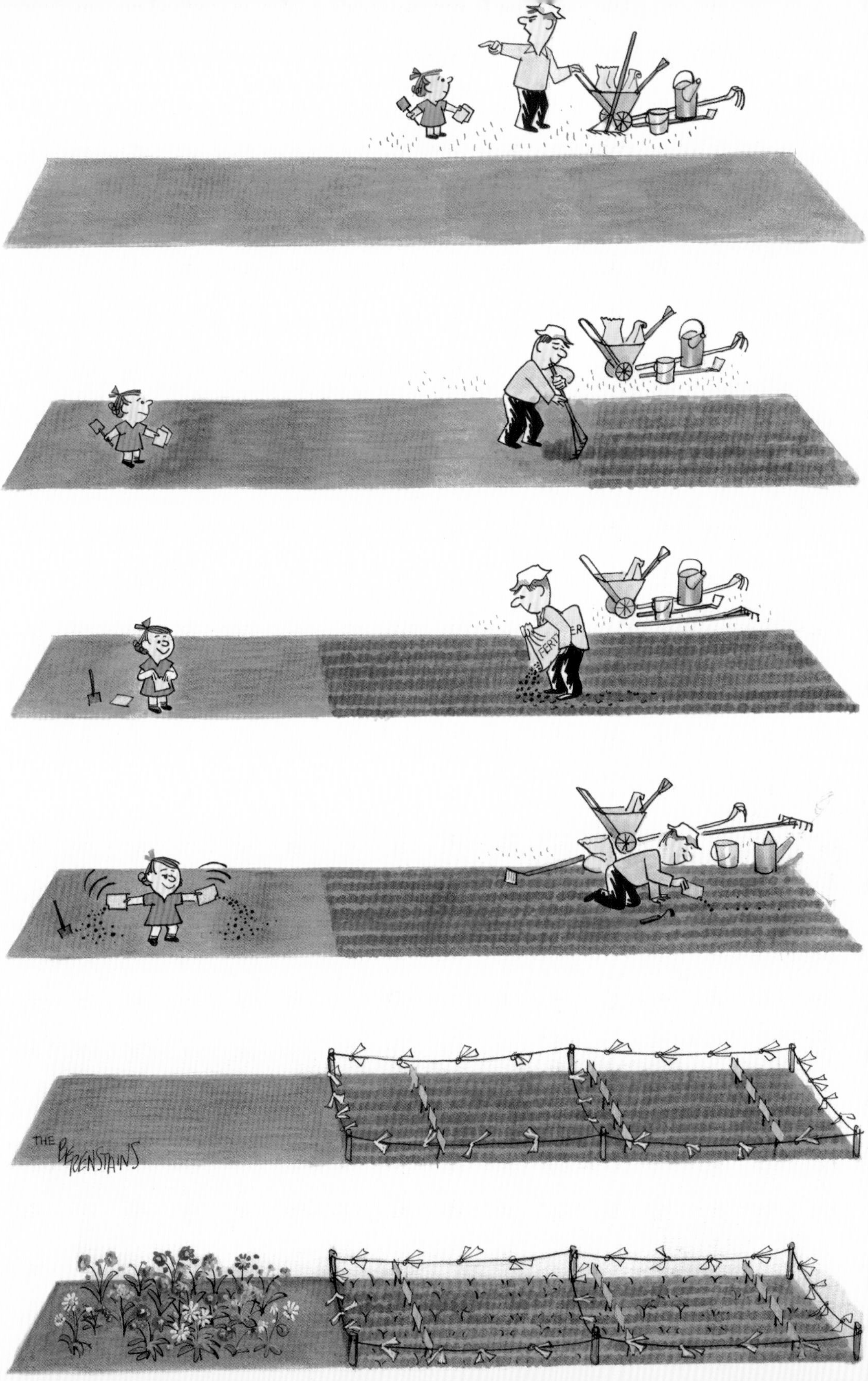
THE BERENSTAINS

e intrepid couple set to work. The

d *Tribune Syndicate* picked up

p and for the whole of 1953 and

and Jan labored in the Dantean

d of the daily comics. The strip

ster highlighted the tomboyish,

aspect of the character who

e ways, a female sibling of

Menace.

STRIP.

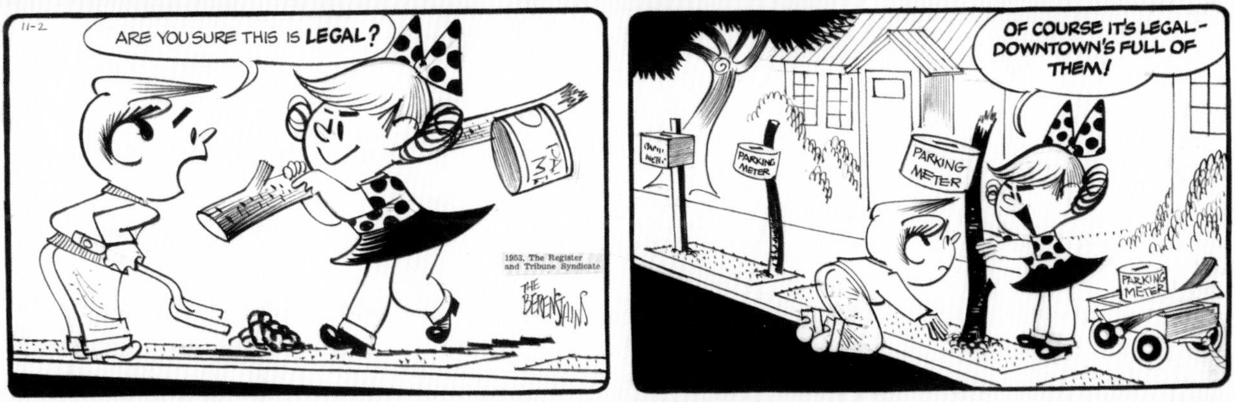
11-2
ARE YOU SURE THIS IS **LEGAL**?
1953, The Register and Tribune Syndicate
THE BERENSTAINS
OF COURSE IT'S LEGAL- DOWNTOWN'S FULL OF THEM!
PARKING METER
PARKING METER
PARKING METER

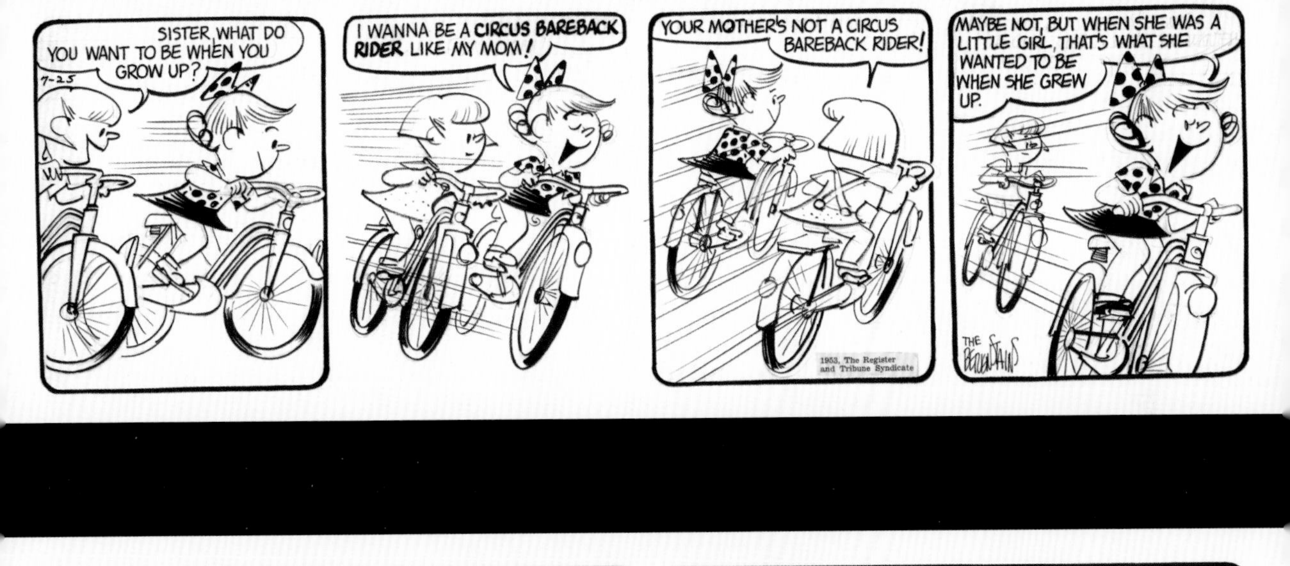
SISTER, WHAT DO YOU WANT TO BE WHEN YOU GROW UP?
7-25
I WANNA BE A **CIRCUS BAREBACK RIDER** LIKE MY MOM!
YOUR MOTHER'S NOT A CIRCUS BAREBACK RIDER!
1953, The Register and Tribune Syndicate
MAYBE NOT, BUT WHEN SHE WAS A LITTLE GIRL, THAT'S WHAT SHE WANTED TO BE WHEN SHE GREW UP.
THE BERENSTAINS

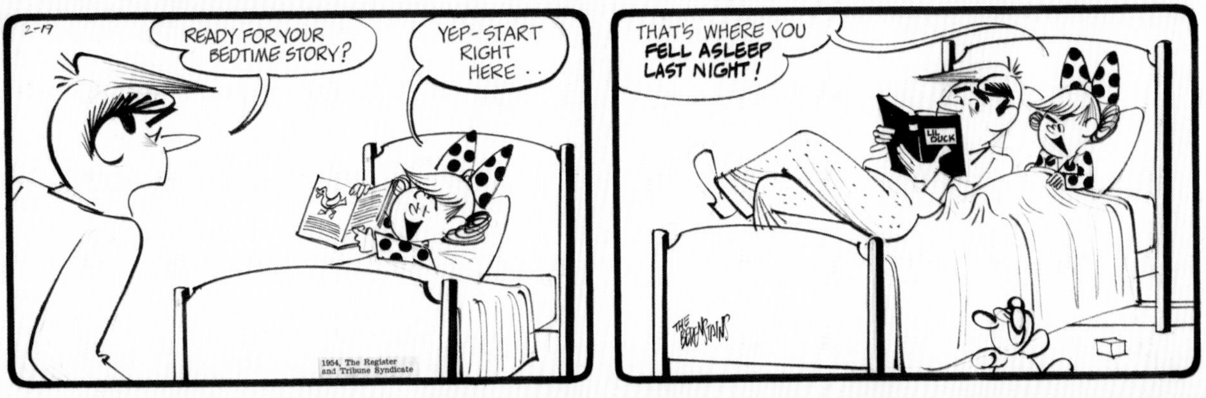
2-19
READY FOR YOUR BEDTIME STORY?
YEP- START RIGHT HERE . .
1954, The Register and Tribune Syndicate
THAT'S WHERE YOU **FELL ASLEEP LAST NIGHT**!
LIL DUCK
THE BERENSTAINS

SISTER! WHAT ARE YOU DOING?

YOU KNOW HOW YOU ALWAYS SAY I HAVE ENOUGH TOYS AT HOME TO START A STORE?...

WELL, I'M IN BUSINESS!

1963, The Register and Tribune Syndicate

THE BERENSTAINS

LEFT! RIGHT! LEFT! RIGHT!

LEFT! RIGHT! ABOU-U-U-T

FACE!!!

???

DO YOU WANNA TAKE YOUR TEDDY BEAR TO BED WITH YOU?

I'D LIKE TO, DAD, ...

- BUT THERE'S NO MORE ROOM!

THE BERENSTAINS

1963, The Register and Tribune Syndicate

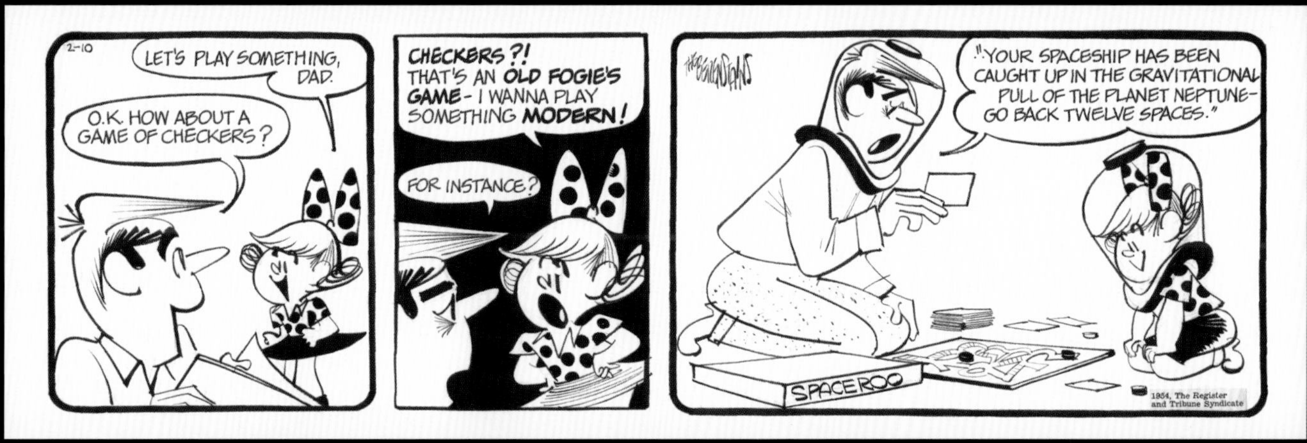
2-10
LET'S PLAY SOMETHING, DAD.
O.K. HOW ABOUT A GAME OF CHECKERS?
CHECKERS?! THAT'S AN OLD FOGIE'S GAME - I WANNA PLAY SOMETHING MODERN!
FOR INSTANCE?
THE BERENSTAINS
"YOUR SPACESHIP HAS BEEN CAUGHT UP IN THE GRAVITATIONAL PULL OF THE PLANET NEPTUNE - GO BACK TWELVE SPACES."
SPACEROO
1954, The Register and Tribune Syndicate

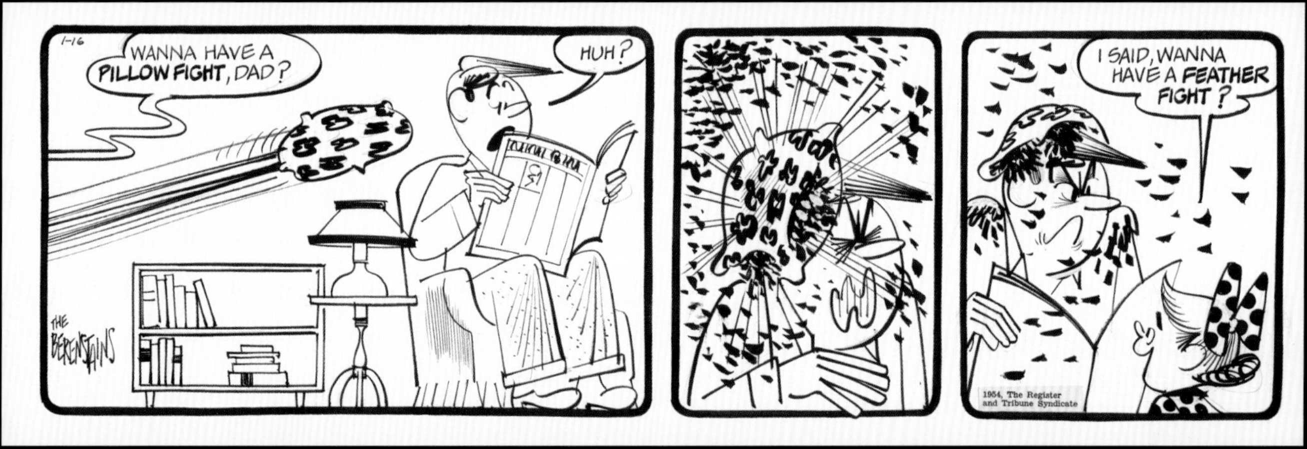
1-16
WANNA HAVE A PILLOW FIGHT, DAD?
HUH?
THE BERENSTAINS
I SAID, WANNA HAVE A FEATHER FIGHT?
1954, The Register and Tribune Syndicate

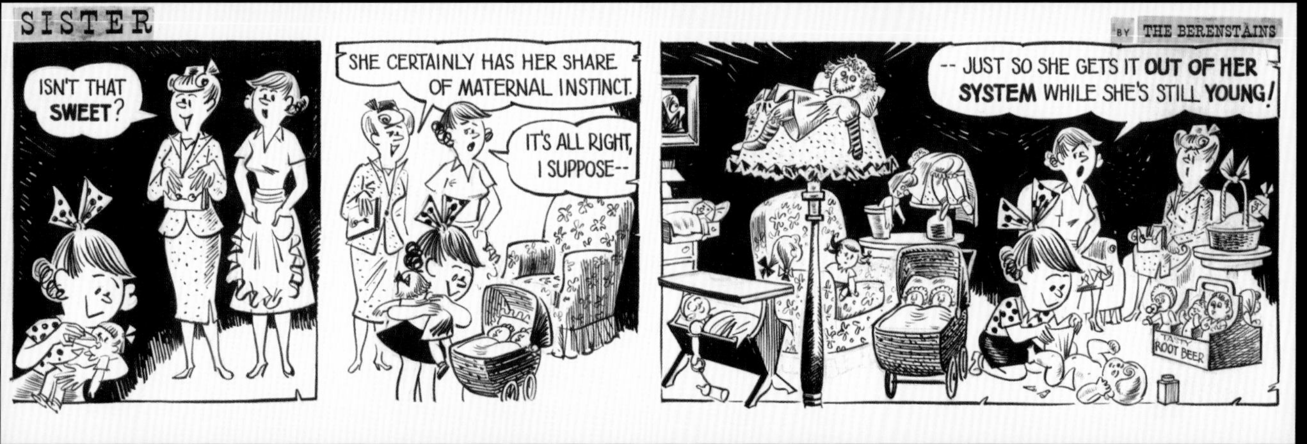
SISTER
BY THE BERENSTAINS
ISN'T THAT SWEET?
SHE CERTAINLY HAS HER SHARE OF MATERNAL INSTINCT.
IT'S ALL RIGHT, I SUPPOSE--
-- JUST SO SHE GETS IT OUT OF HER SYSTEM WHILE SHE'S STILL YOUNG!
TASTY ROOT BEER

In the *Sister* Sunday features, Stan
and Jan were able to loosen up with some
elaborate and ambitious comic art. They were
also able to explore more complex subject
matter and follow up on their baby book
successes by offering a little parenting advice.

SISTER; SUNDAY FEATURES, 1953–1954

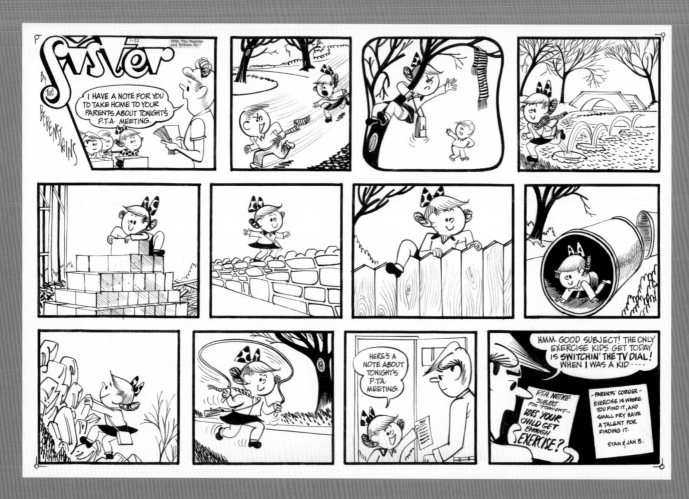

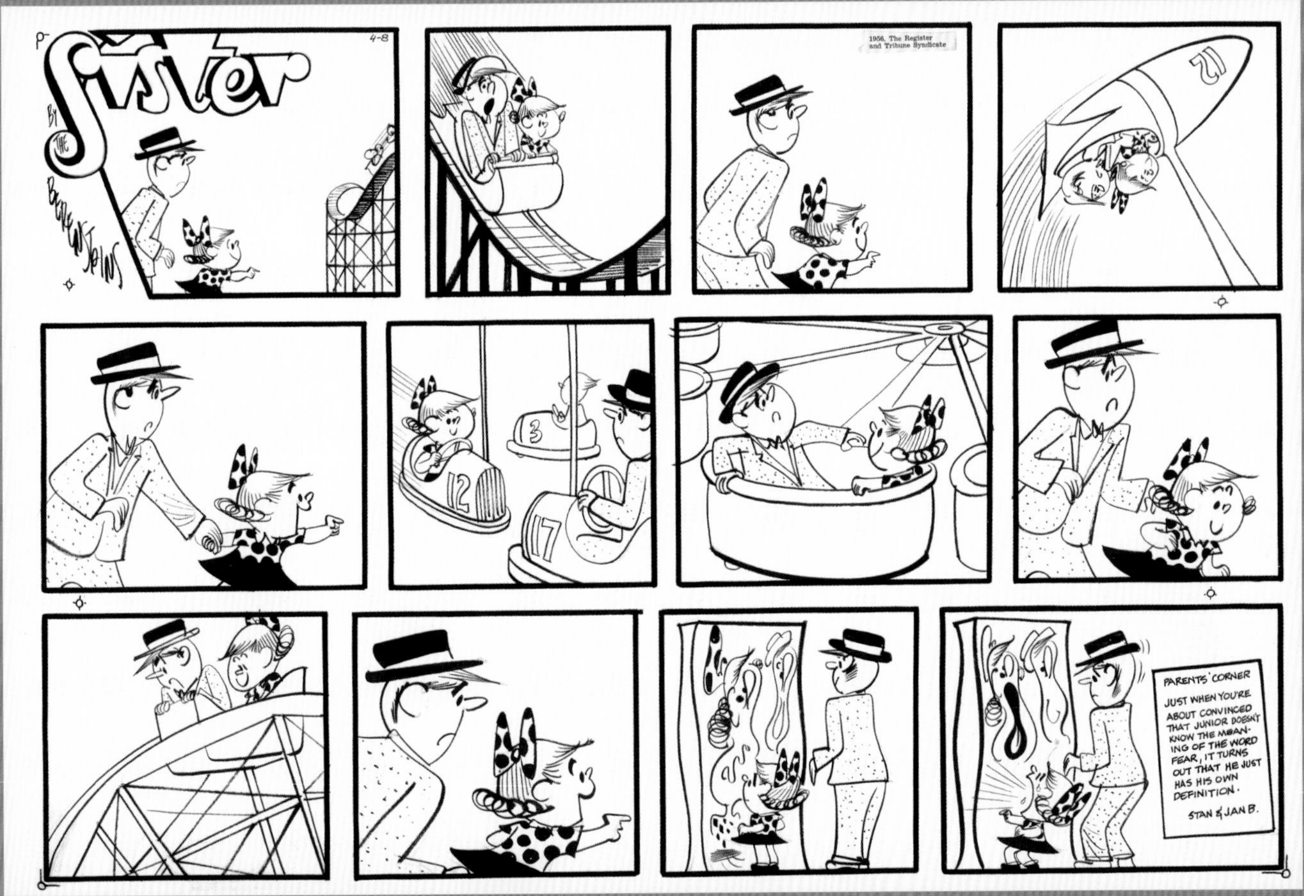
Sister
By the Berenstains
4-8
1956, The Register
and Tribune Syndicate
12
3
12
17
PARENTS' CORNER
JUST WHEN YOU'RE ABOUT CONVINCED THAT JUNIOR DOESN'T KNOW THE MEAN-ING OF THE WORD FEAR, IT TURNS OUT THAT HE JUST HAS HIS OWN DEFINITION.
STAN & JAN B.

4-18
Sister
LET'S START PUTTING YOUR SOAP-BOX CAR TOGETHER
WAIT A MINUTE
WE DON'T HAVE A SOAP BOX
THAT'S NO PROBLEM. WELL GET ONE FROM THE GROCER.
JUST ANY OLD BOX WON'T DO.
WHY NOT? A BOX IS A BOX.
BOXES? THERE'S A LOAD OF 'EM OUT BACK.
GROCERY
NOPE. NONE OF THESE'LL DO.
WHAT DIFFERENCE DOES IT MAKE?
IT MAKES A LOT OF DIFFERENCE!
SOAP
THIS IS RIDICULOUS! ANYONE OF THESE WILL DO FINE.
HERE'S A DANDY ONE!
IT JUST WON'T DO!
WELL, WHAT KIND OF BOX WILL DO?
YOU'LL SEE.
LET'S TRY THE SUPER MARKET.
THAT'S THE ONE I WANT!
NOW, MAYBE YOU'LL TELL ME WHY YOU HAD TO HAVE THIS PARTICULAR BOX.
OH, I JUST HAD MY LI'L OLE HEART SET ON A FOREIGN CAR
IMPORTED CASTILE SOAP

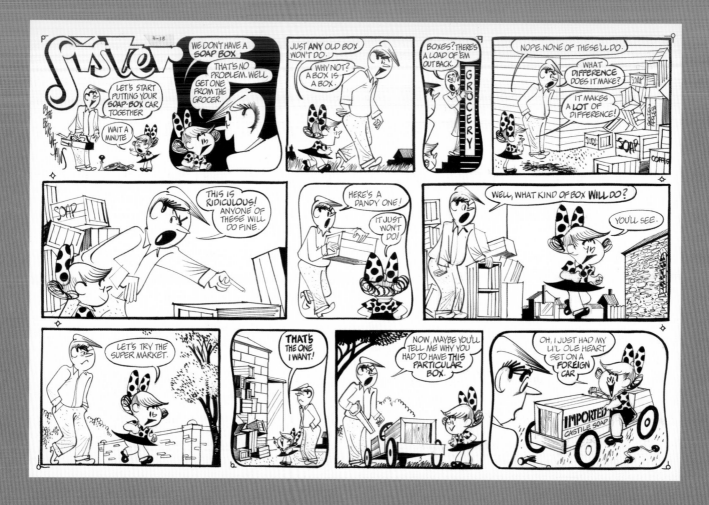

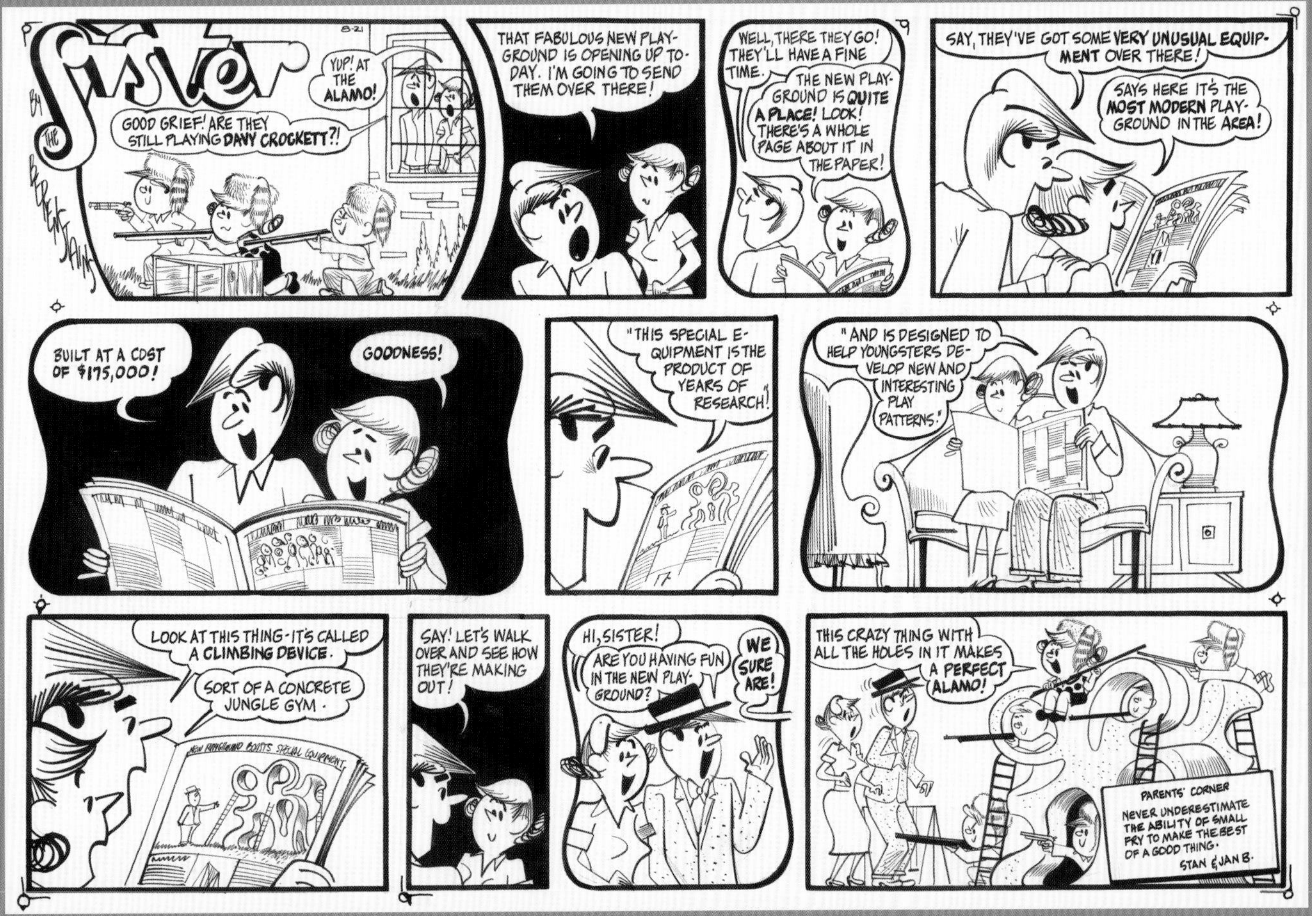
Sister
By The Berenstains
8-21
GOOD GRIEF! ARE THEY STILL PLAYING DAVY CROCKETT?!
YUP! AT THE ALAMO!
THAT FABULOUS NEW PLAY-GROUND IS OPENING UP TO-DAY. I'M GOING TO SEND THEM OVER THERE!
WELL, THERE THEY GO! THEY'LL HAVE A FINE TIME.
THE NEW PLAY-GROUND IS QUITE A PLACE! LOOK! THERE'S A WHOLE PAGE ABOUT IT IN THE PAPER!
SAY, THEY'VE GOT SOME VERY UNUSUAL EQUIP-MENT OVER THERE!
SAYS HERE IT'S THE MOST MODERN PLAY-GROUND IN THE AREA!
BUILT AT A COST OF $175,000!
GOODNESS!
"THIS SPECIAL E-QUIPMENT IS THE PRODUCT OF YEARS OF RESEARCH!"
"AND IS DESIGNED TO HELP YOUNGSTERS DE-VELOP NEW AND INTERESTING PLAY PATTERNS."
LOOK AT THIS THING - IT'S CALLED A CLIMBING DEVICE.
SORT OF A CONCRETE JUNGLE GYM.
SAY! LET'S WALK OVER AND SEE HOW THEY'RE MAKING OUT!
HI, SISTER!
ARE YOU HAVING FUN IN THE NEW PLAY-GROUND?
WE SURE ARE!
THIS CRAZY THING WITH ALL THE HOLES IN IT MAKES A PERFECT ALAMO!
PARENTS' CORNER
NEVER UNDERESTIMATE THE ABILITY OF SMALL FRY TO MAKE THE BEST OF A GOOD THING.
STAN & JAN B.

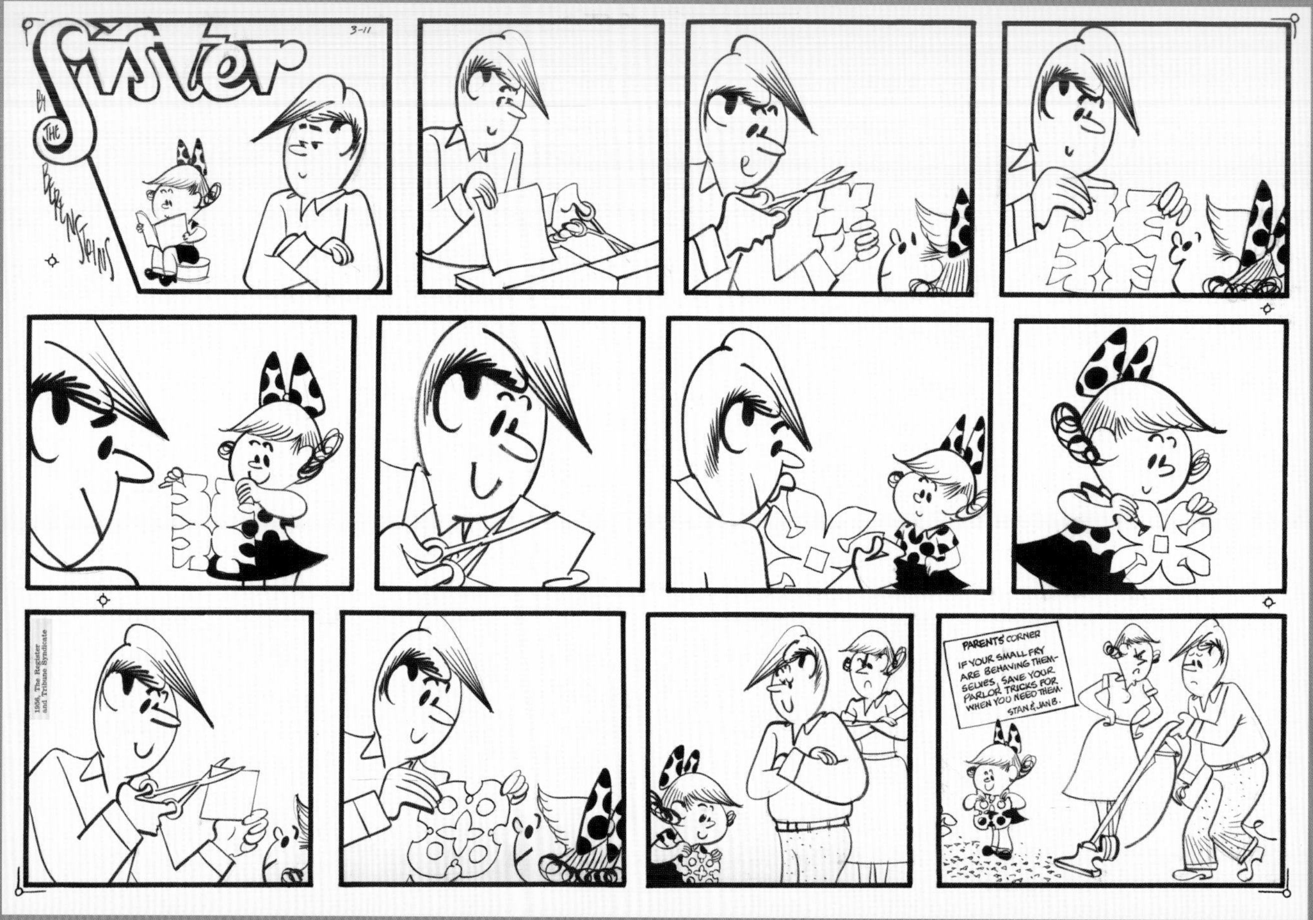
Sister
BY THE BERENSTAINS
3-11
1956, The Register and Tribune Syndicate
PARENTS' CORNER
IF YOUR SMALL FRY ARE BEHAVING THEM-SELVES, SAVE YOUR PARLOR TRICKS FOR WHEN YOU NEED THEM.
STAN & JAN B.

Sister
DARN OLE RAIN!
WHY DON'T YOU TRY OUT THAT FUNBOOK I GOT YOU?
3-7
YOU'LL LOVE THIS. YOU JUST DRAW A LINE FROM ONE NUMBER TO THE NEXT, AND IT MAKES A PICTURE!
WHERE DO YOU START?
AT NUMBER ONE, OF COURSE
WHERE DO I GO FROM THERE?
TWO!
WHERE DO I GO FROM TWO?
TRY THREE.
BETCHA FOUR IS NEXT.
THA-A-A-TS RIGHT.
DADDY!
WHAT NOW?!
I CAN'T FIND FOUR.
YOU'VE GOT YOUR THUMB ON IT!
FUN BOOK
IS THIS RIGHT SO FAR?
1954, The Register and Tribune Syndicate
NO. IT'S NOT. YOU'RE SKIPPING NUMBERS!
FUN
HERE. I MADE YOU A CHART. FOLLOW THIS AND IT'LL MAKE A PICTURE.
1. 2. 3. 4. 5. 6.
7. 8. 9. 10. 11. 12.
IT DIDN'T MAKE MUCH OF A PICTURE.
NO NO NO THAT'S JUST A GUIDE!
HEY, LOOK! THE RAIN STOPPED! HERE-YOU FINISH IT!

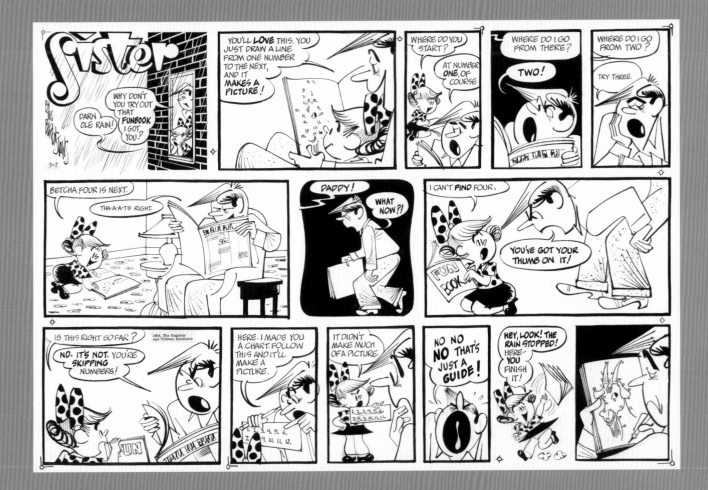

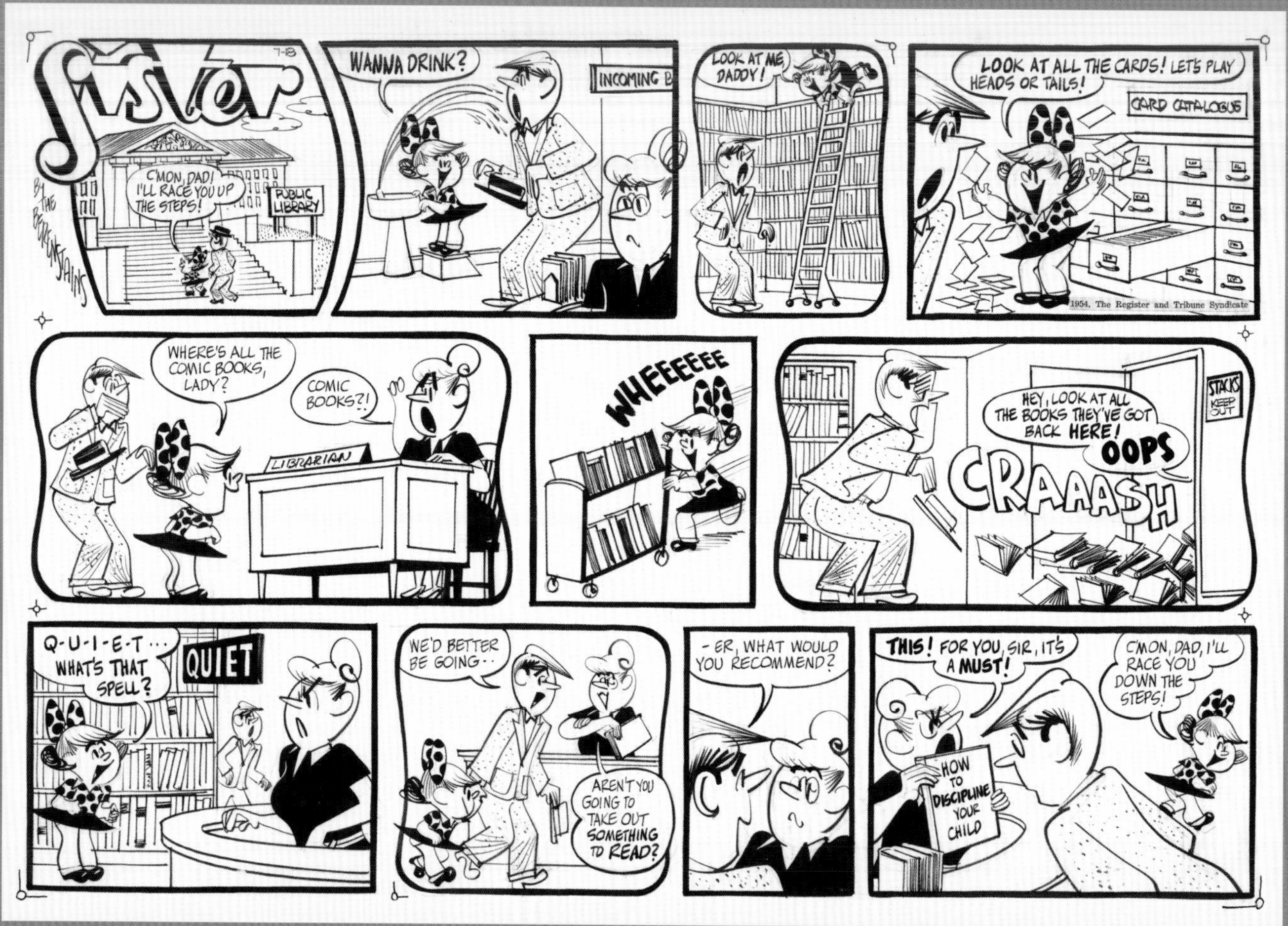
Sister
BY THE BORKENSTEINS
7-18
C'MON, DAD! I'LL RACE YOU UP THE STEPS!
PUBLIC LIBRARY
WANNA DRINK?
INCOMING B
LOOK AT ME, DADDY!
LOOK AT ALL THE CARDS! LET'S PLAY HEADS OR TAILS!
CARD CATALOGUE
1954, The Register and Tribune Syndicate
WHERE'S ALL THE COMIC BOOKS, LADY?
COMIC BOOKS?!
LIBRARIAN
WHEEEEEE
HEY, LOOK AT ALL THE BOOKS THEY'VE GOT BACK HERE!
OOPS
STACKS KEEP OUT
CRAAASH
Q-U-I-E-T... WHAT'S THAT SPELL?
QUIET
WE'D BETTER BE GOING..
AREN'T YOU GOING TO TAKE OUT SOMETHING TO READ?
- ER, WHAT WOULD YOU RECOMMEND?
THIS! FOR YOU, SIR, IT'S A MUST!
HOW TO DISCIPLINE YOUR CHILD
C'MON, DAD, I'LL RACE YOU DOWN THE STEPS!

Sister
2-13
BY THE BERENSTAINS
EVENING PLAY HOUR?!.. WHAT FOR? SHE PLAYS ALL DAY!
THAT'S NOT THE IDEA. THE POINT IS THAT A CHILD HER AGE NEEDS TO SPEND SOME TIME WITH HER FATHER
SISTER, STARTING TONIGHT YOU AND DADDY ARE GOING TO HAVE A REGULAR EVENING PLAY-HOUR
OH, THE JOYS OF PARENT-HOOD.
WHAT DO YOU WANT TO PLAY, DADDY?
TELL YOU WHAT - LET'S PLAY FARM YARD. I'LL BE THE GOAT!
UMM. I DON'T THINK SO.
WE COULD GET YOUR DOLLS!
I DON'T FEEL LIKE DOLLS.
HOW ABOUT BUILDING STUFF OUT OF BLOCKS?
TIRED OF BLOCKS.
LET'S THINK OF SOMETHING THAT'S REALLY FUN.
TIDDLY-WINKS?
NAAA
CHECKERS?
NAAA
PARCHESI?
NAAA.
I KNOW WHAT! WE'LL HAVE A JIG-SAW PUZZLE TOURNAMENT!
WHAT'S THAT?
1955, The Register and Tribune Syndicate
WE EACH HAVE A JIG-SAW PUZZLE - THEN WE BOTH START AT THE SAME TIME, AND WHOEVER GETS FINISHED FIRST, WINS!
READY? GO!
MINE'S DONE! I WIN!
WHA-?... I JUST GOT STARTED. LET'S MAKE IT BEST OUT OF THREE.
MINE'S DONE! I WIN!
WELL, I'LL BE - LET'S MAKE IT BEST OUT OF FIVE!
GEE, I'M SORRY, DAD, BUT YOU'LL HAVE TO WAIT UNTIL TOMORROW NIGHT - YOUR HOUR'S UP!
PARENTS' CORNER
GIVE THE EVENING PLAY HOUR IDEA HALF A CHANCE AND IT MAY PROVE TO BE ONE OF THE HIGH SPOTS OF YOUR DAY.
STAN & JAN B.

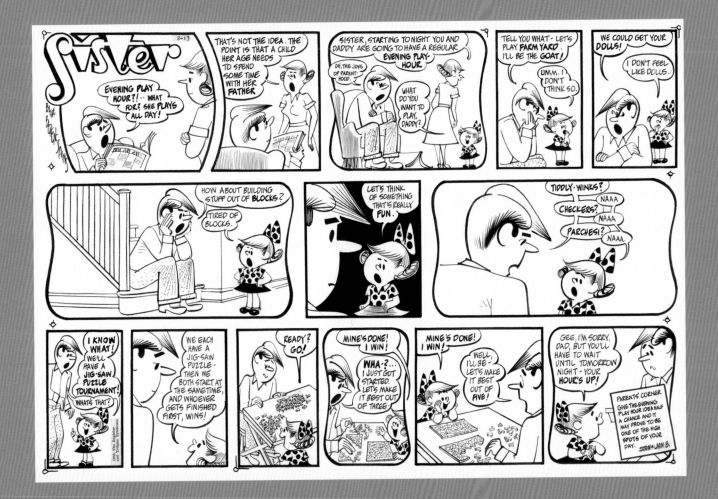

Sister
BY THE BERENSTAINS
10-2
DADDY··
KALEIDOSCOPE
1955, The Register and Tribune Syndicate
HOW DOES THIS KALEIDOSCOPE WORK?
WAIT 'TIL I FINISH TALKING ON THE PHONE -
BE HAPPY TO EXPLAIN IT TO YOU, DEAR···
···THERE ARE SIX LITTLE CARFLE WHEELS WHICH WORK WITH THE KRANASTAT··
··· HERE, I'LL SHOW YOU ON THE BLACKBOARD···
··· HERE'S YOUR EYE···
··· AND HERE ARE THE VARIOUS PINDLE COGS···
··· AS YOU TURN THE KALEIDOSCOPE THE CARFLE WHEELS FALL INTO PLACE···
··THIS DIAGRAM SHOWS THE TOGGLE KLATCH···
··· AND WE MUSTN'T FORGET THE REVOLVING RATCH FOBS···
NOW, WHAT WAS THAT YOU WANTED TO KNOW, SISTER?
CARFLE WHEELS
KRANASTAT
RATCH FOBS
ER, NOTHING, DAD. NOTHING AT ALL - REALLY, NOTHING AT ALL!
PARENTS' CORNER
WHEN YOU'RE CALLED UPON TO PLAY "ANSWER MAN" KEEP YOUR ANSWERS SHORT, SWEET AND TO THE POINT - ONE LONG-WINDED HARANGUE CAN SCARE A KID OUT OF A YEAR'S HEALTHY CURIOSITY.
STAN & JAN B.

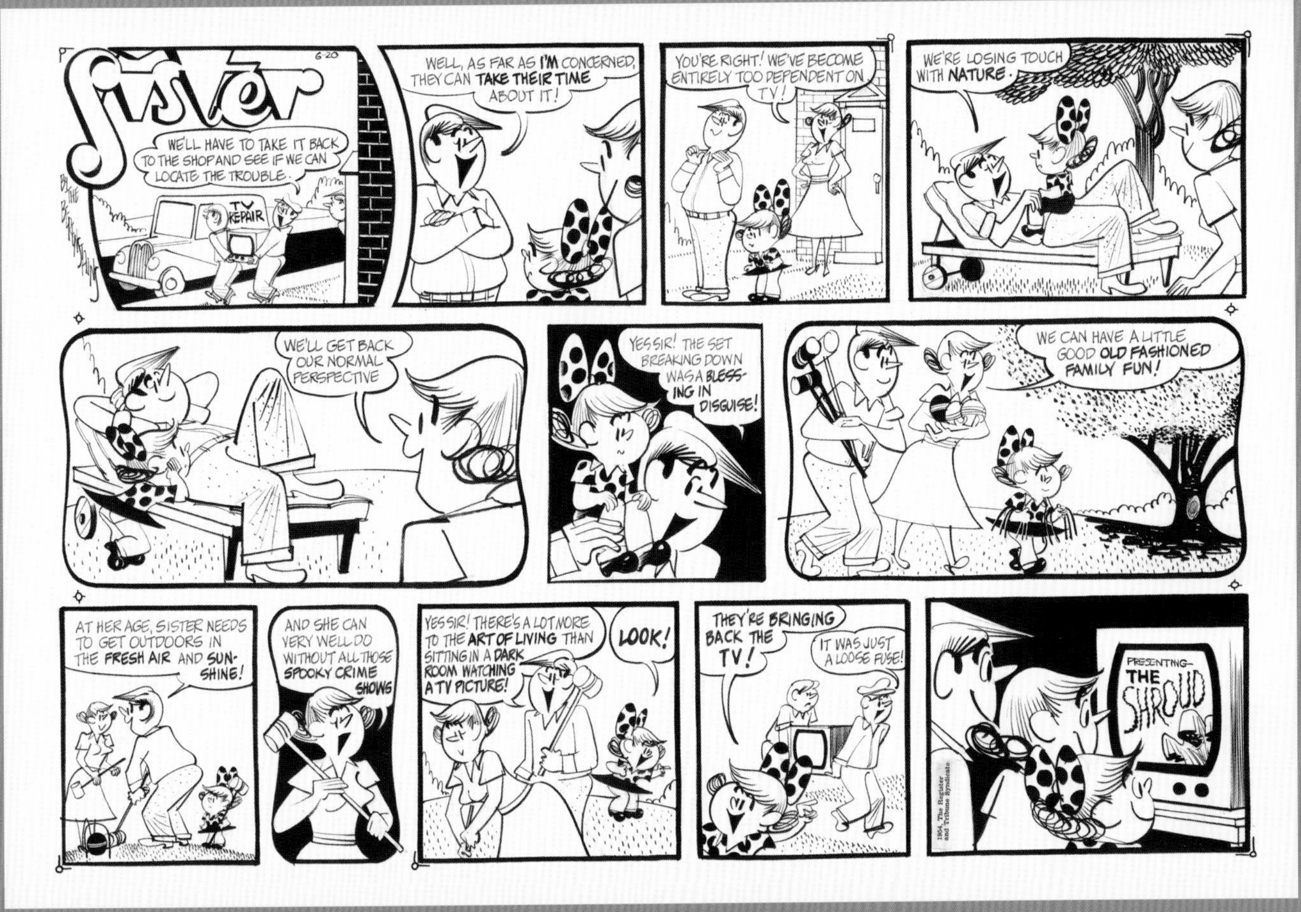
Sister
6-20
WE'LL HAVE TO TAKE IT BACK TO THE SHOP AND SEE IF WE CAN LOCATE THE TROUBLE.
TV REPAIR
WELL, AS FAR AS I'M CONCERNED, THEY CAN TAKE THEIR TIME ABOUT IT!
YOU'RE RIGHT! WE'VE BECOME ENTIRELY TOO DEPENDENT ON TV!
WE'RE LOSING TOUCH WITH NATURE.
WE'LL GET BACK OUR NORMAL PERSPECTIVE
YES SIR! THE SET BREAKING DOWN WAS A BLESSING IN DISGUISE!
WE CAN HAVE A LITTLE GOOD OLD FASHIONED FAMILY FUN!
AT HER AGE, SISTER NEEDS TO GET OUTDOORS IN THE FRESH AIR AND SUNSHINE!
AND SHE CAN VERY WELL DO WITHOUT ALL THOSE SPOOKY CRIME SHOWS
YES SIR! THERE'S A LOT MORE TO THE ART OF LIVING THAN SITTING IN A DARK ROOM WATCHING A TV PICTURE!
LOOK!
THEY'RE BRINGING BACK THE TV!
IT WAS JUST A LOOSE FUSE!
PRESENTING— THE SHROUD
1954, The Register and Tribune Syndicate

Though similar in some ways to *Dennis*, *Sister* did not resemble the Menace in the extent of its newspaper distribution. The plain fact was that, in spite of all their efforts, it was not paying off. After about seven hundred drawings, Stan and Jan decided that the newspaper business was not for them. They fled, sweat-soaked and ink-stained, not much richer but a little wiser, back into the welcoming arms of *Collier's,* who happily, reintroduced their work in the original format they had pioneered: full-page feature cartoons.

BACK TO SCHOOL; *COLLIER'S*; SEPTEMBER 16, 1955

SUPERMARKET; COLLIER'S, NOVEMBER, 1955

One of these features had a special appeal for me at the time. *Toy Department*, a compendium of new toys, which illustrated an article about the toy industry's latest offerings, appeared on my fifth birthday, December 21, 1956. I well remember drooling over this wonderful array of desirable toys as my parents created it and wondering which ones I might be getting for my birthday or Christmas (I didn't care which). Being a true child of the 1950s, I particularly coveted the gigantic artillery piece though it made no appearance on Christmas morning. I do think I got the little rocket-firing spaceman and I certainly had that twirly bubble-maker at some point. That's my rocking horse, too, in the upper left.

TOY DEPARTMENT; COLLIER'S; DECEMBER 21, 1956

One of Stan and Jan's last *Collier's* pieces featured two new crazes on the American pop culture scene. *Space Show*, presciently published the year before Sputnik, is a charming look at the early days of outer space mania. Toy spaceships, ray guns, and space helmets are pictured while, there, lurking gray and ghostly in the corner, is the source of coming trouble, that most characteristic institution of all fiftiesdom— television!

SPACE SHOW; COLLIER'S, 1956

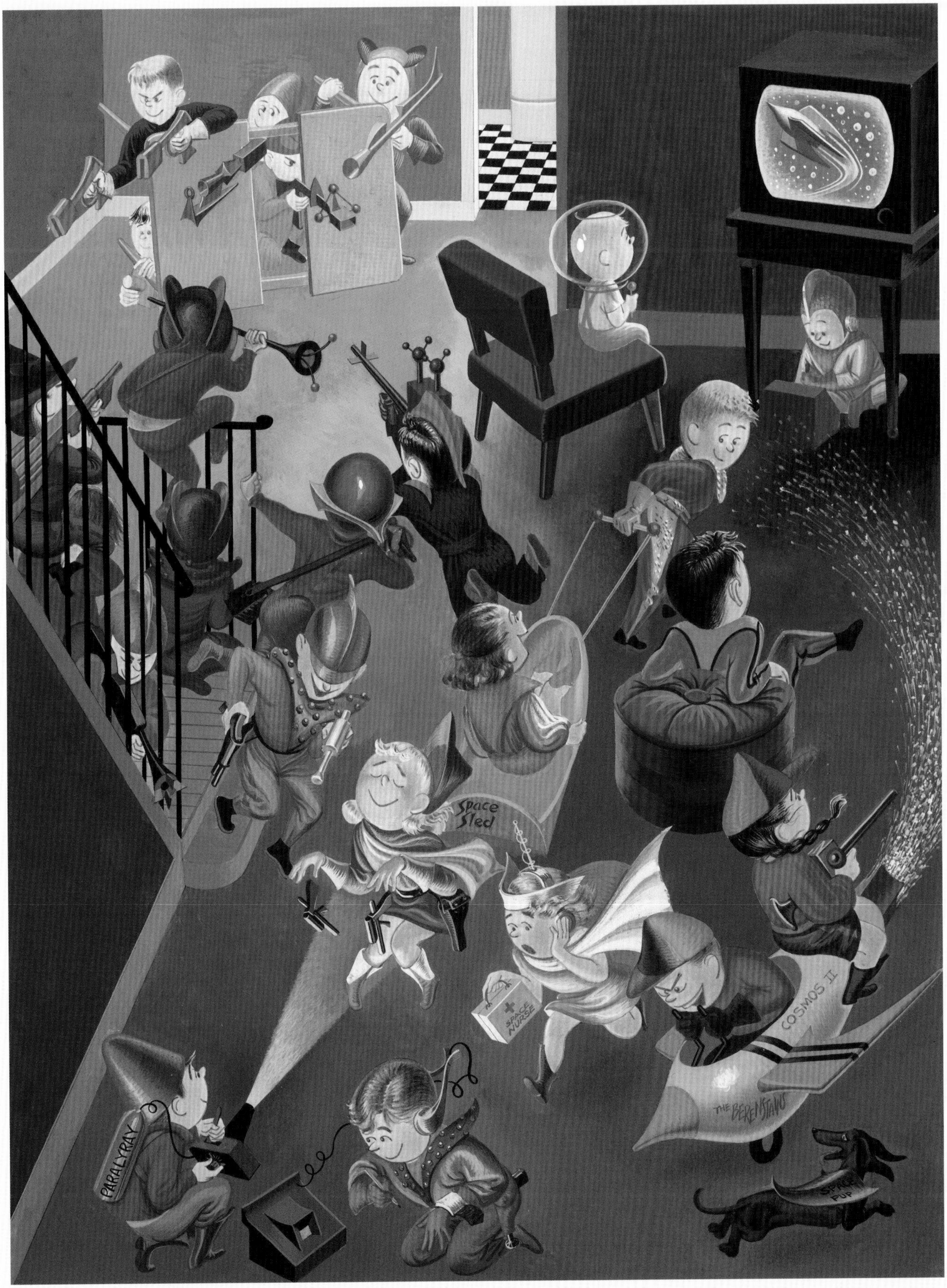
Space Sled
SPACE NURSE
COSMOS II
THE BERENSTAINS
SPACE PUP
PARALYRAY

The explosive popularity of the new medium rang the death knell of the general interest weekly magazine. Folks were not content to sit around reading stodgy articles by Lowell Thomas or genteel stories by A. J. Cronin when they could partake of the wild hilarity of Uncle Milty or Sid Caesar on the dimly luminous tube. *The Saturday Evening Post* survived in truncated form by going from weekly to monthly publication. But *Collier's* went under. It ceased publication at the end of 1956.

Surprisingly, Stan and Jan survived this catastrophic loss of their principle source of income quite nimbly. One area of magazine publishing that continued to thrive in the new multimedia era was the venerable monthly woman's magazine. *Redbook*, *Ladies' Home Journal*, *Good Housekeeping*, and *McCall's* had been around since the turn of the century and were showing no signs of going the way of the buggy whip. Stan and Jan shifted their focus to this alternate venue and thrived.

McCall's quickly snapped up their new series, *It's All in the Family* (no connection to the later TV sitcom), which graced its pages from 1956 to the new-broom regime of Shana Alexander in the early seventies when it migrated to *Good Housekeeping*, where it continued until 1988. This feature, in fact, lasted so long that for the final few years of its existence it was ghost-written and drawn by yours truly.

It's All in the Family took the mom, the dad, and the daughter from *Sister*, bookended the girl between an older and younger brother, and settled them down in a Leave-it-to-Beaverish suburbia tailored to the traditionally domestic *McCall's*. These kids, by the way, had "real" names: Michael, Janie, and Billy. They even had a last name: the Harveys.

"I have four—a boy three and a half, a girl five, a boy seven and a husband thirty-five.";
TRIP TO TOYLAND; *IT'S ALL IN THE FAMILY; McCALL'S;* DECEMBER 1957

It's All in the Family dealt with many of the traditional childhood themes that Stan and Jan had already visited, like making mud pies.

"AI-IEEEeeeeeeeeee-e-AI!";
WEEKEND; *IT'S ALL IN THE FAMILY;* **McCALL'S; AUGUST 1960**

"You said to make friends.";
NEW NEIGHBORS; *IT'S ALL IN THE FAMILY;* **McCALL'S; APRIL 1960**

"Okay, you can turn the water on.";
BATHTIME; *IT'S ALL IN THE FAMILY;* **McCALL'S; MARCH 1957**

"That was A. Now here's B-flat."; MUSIC HATH CHARMS; *IT'S ALL IN THE FAMILY*; McCALL'S; NOVEMBER 1958

"There's so much it can give her—grace,
poise, femininity . . . ."; BALLERINA;
IT'S ALL IN THE FAMILY; McCALL'S; OCTOBER 1962

HOMEWORK; *IT'S ALL IN THE FAMILY*; *McCALL'S*; MAY 1956

"Thath all right. It was looth, anyway.";
HALLOWEEN PARTY; *IT'S ALL IN THE FAMILY*;
McCALL'S; OCTOBER 1959

This feature—seven panel cartoons or more on a single theme once a month for thirty-two years—became the background to our family life while my brother and I were growing up. The fact is that I identify with these characters more closely than the infinitely better-known Berenstain Bears. People often ask if I am "Brother Bear." I never bother to explain that I am actually "Billy" of the Harvey family—an obscure remark, at best. Each *It's All in the Family* feature was a little story taken from my own experience. My (temporary) obsession with dinosaurs, for instance, was immediately seized upon and turned into cartoons.

**DINOSAURS; *IT'S ALL IN THE FAMILY*; *McCALL'S*;
JANUARY 1962**

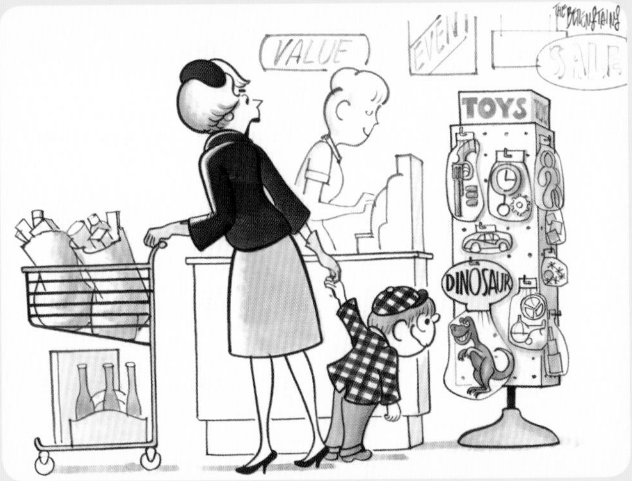
VALUE
TOYS
DINOSAURS

"Come on, Billy, mother's all checked out . . . Billy . . . BILLY . . . "

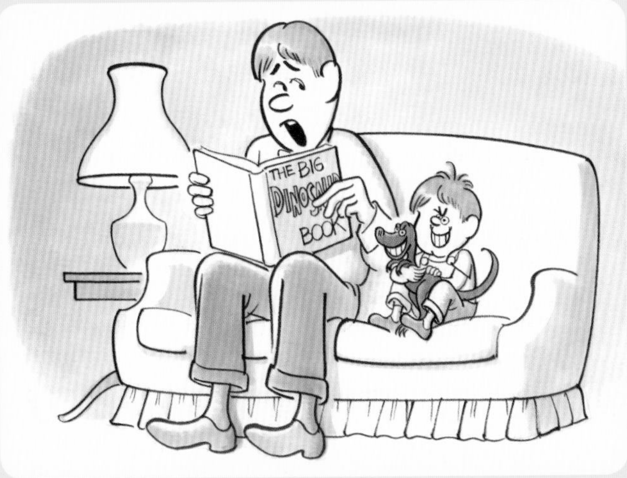
THE BIG
DINOSAUR
BOOK

"The fiercest of the giant carnivores was the King Tyrant Lizard. He roamed the earth, killing and eating every creature that came within his grasp."

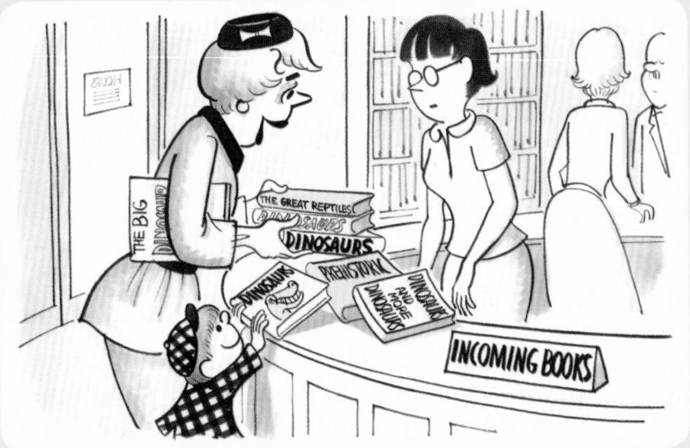
THE BIG
THE GREAT REPTILES
DINOSAURS
PREHISTORY
INCOMING BOOKS

"We'd like to renew these, please."

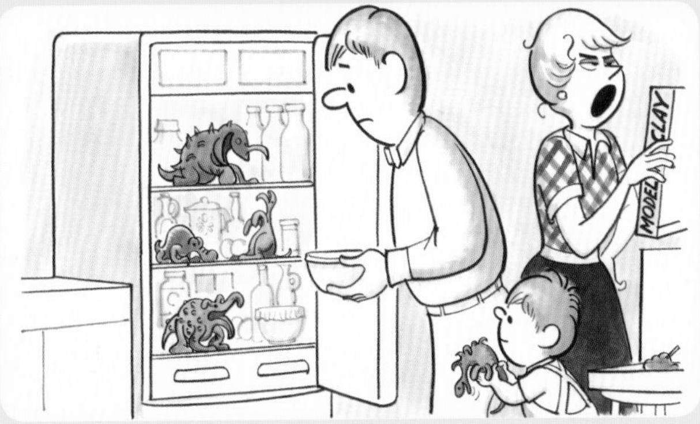
MODEL
CLAY

"May be returned to firmness by placing temporarily in a cool place.'"

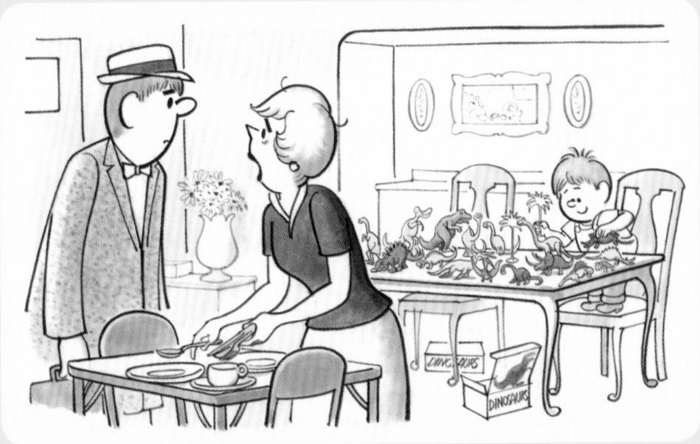
DINOSAURS

"I hope you don't mind dinner on the card table."

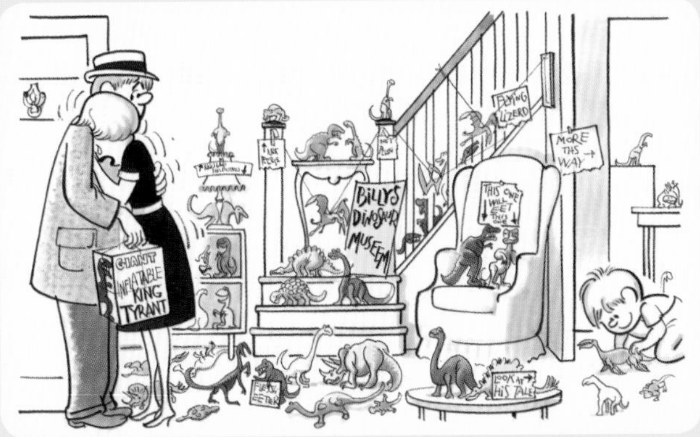
GIANT
INFLATABLE
KING
TYRANT
BILLY'S
DINOSAUR
MUSEUM
FLYING LIZARD
MORE THIS WAY

"Wherever I look, wherever I walk, wherever I sit—."

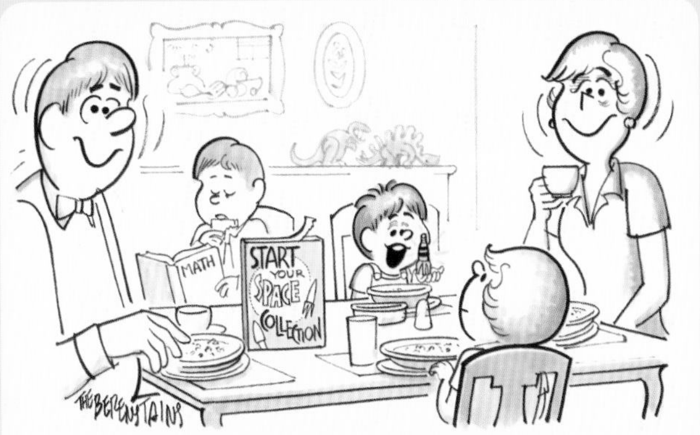
MATH
START YOUR SPACE COLLECTION

"Hey, look at this nifty space capsule that came with the cereal!"

I think it was my older brother, Leo's, attempts to master a two-wheeler that provided the model for the girl of the family's bike riding experiences—though he, no doubt, dispensed with the stylish beret.

TWO-WHEELER; *IT'S ALL IN THE FAMILY*; McCALL'S; JANUARY 1959

"There's nothing difficult about riding a two-wheeler. It's all just a matter of . . . ."

"They respond to the slightest pressure."

"b-b-balance . . . Another thing you have to learn is . . . ."

"This little packet under the seat is a tool kit."

"how to stop . . . You have to be careful with these hand brakes."

"There! Now you give 'er a try. Daddy'll be right beside you."

Fans of the Berenstain Bears books will recognize in this little tale of a father's tribulations in teaching his child to ride a bike the origins of Stan and Jan's second children's book, *The Berenstain Bears' Bike Lesson*. They may also recognize, in incipient form, the persona of Papa Bear—a well-meaning and devoted father who is somewhat accident-prone and liable to over-confidence—perhaps, even, to a little pomposity and self-importance.

Many have assumed that some nefarious intent lay behind this depiction of the institution of American Fatherhood. But I can assure them that the image of Dad and Mom that was created was purely autobiographical. My father and mother really were a lot like Papa Bear and Mama Bear. After all, they always tell you to write about what you know.

"'Little League rules shall be identical with official baseball rules with the following exceptions . . .'"

LITTLE LEAGUE; *IT'S ALL IN THE FAMILY*; McCALL'S; JULY 1959

"All right, so you didn't come in first, second, third or fourth. But look at it this way—
simply to have run a mile at all is a tremendous feat.";

FIELD DAY; *IT'S ALL IN THE FAMILY*; *McCALL'S*; MAY 1958

"All right, so you didn't come in first, second, third or fourth. But look at it this way—
simply to have taken part in the sack race at all . . . ";

FIELD DAY; *IT'S ALL IN THE FAMILY;* McCALLS ; MAY 1958

"And so, as the hare slept, the tortoise kept up a slow, steady pace.'";

FAVORITE UNCLE; *IT'S ALL IN THE FAMILY*; *McCALL'S*; SEPTEMBER 1964

UNPUBLISHED SKETCH FOR "THE NEST;" *IT'S ALL IN THE FAMILY; McCALL'S;* 1963

"Well, that was okay for a starter.";

AMUSEMENT PARK; *IT'S ALL IN THE FAMILY;* **McCALL'S; SEPTEMBER 1957**

"Hey! Look! Oh, boy! Wowee! Oh, boy!";

AMUSEMENT PARK; *IT'S ALL IN THE FAMILY*; *McCALL'S*; SEPTEMBER 1957

The mother of this cartoon family exhibits some of the calm, wise, and sensible demeanor of the later Mama Bear though she is slightly more prone to comic misadventure than her ursine descendant.

"Honey, I know your nose hurts, but a bad hop is something that can happen to anybody.";

MINOR LEAGUER; *IT'S ALL IN THE FAMILY; McCALL'S;* MAY 1964

"The pitcher definitely committed a balk. He distinctly began his pitching motion before he threw to first.";

MINOR LEAGUER; *IT'S ALL IN THE FAMILY; McCALL'S;* MAY 1964

"What junk?";

SPRING CLEANING; *IT'S ALL IN THE FAMILY; McCALL'S;* **MARCH 1958**

"But it's going to be hours, yet, till they start the fireworks!";

GLORIOUS FOURTH; *IT'S ALL IN THE FAMILY*; *McCALL'S*; JULY 1960

GLORIOUS FOURTH; *IT'S ALL IN THE FAMILY*; *McCALL'S*; JULY 1960

"I don't know what came over me. Everyone was shouting, 'Slide!', so I slid.";

LAST DAY PICNIC; *IT'S ALL IN THE FAMILY*; *McCALL'S*; JUNE 1964

Sometimes, though, the patience of this particular fictional mom tends to wear a bit thin. In fact she can, at times, be downright stressed-out or even out of control.

"Parents can ease sibling tension by encouraging each child to have his own friends";

SIBLING RIVALRIES; *IT'S ALL IN THE FAMILY*; McCALL'S; SEPTEMBER 1958

"If you are faced with a sibling situation in which there are genuinely clashing personalities,
it is best to be realistic and keep the children apart.";

SIBLING RIVALRIES; *IT'S ALL IN THE FAMILY*; *McCALL'S*; SEPTEMBER 1958

"He seems to understand that Little Clocks run down and is very good about rest time.";

REPORT CARD; *IT'S ALL IN THE FAMILY;* **McCALL'S; NOVEMBER 1957**

"Isn't it terrific, Mom? There's kids here from as far away as Gillespie Street!";

BACK-YARD CIRCUS; *IT'S ALL IN THE FAMILY*; *McCALL'S*; MAY 1960

HOME SICK; *IT'S ALL IN THE FAMILY*; *McCALL'S*; JANUARY 1957

"An occasional fling with "fun foods" adds variety to the feeding program.";

FEEDING TIME; *IT'S ALL IN THE FAMILY*; *McCALL'S*; APRIL 1957

You don't know how I envy you having the time to play with the girls every week.";

BROWNIE MEETING; *IT'S ALL IN THE FAMILY; McCALL'S;* FEBRUARY 1962

"Mom, you're a genius.";

CHRISTMAS PARTY; *IT'S ALL IN THE FAMILY*; *McCALL'S*; DECEMBER 1964

"ATTA BABY! THAT'S THE WAY TO GET THOSE REBOUNDS!";

BASKETBALL; *IT'S ALL IN THE FAMILY*; *McCALL'S*; JANUARY 1963

"All right. Now that everyone has seen Billy's mother in the tree—";

PTA FAIR; *IT'S ALL IN THE FAMILY*; *McCALL'S*; JUNE 1964

"Imagine being married to that!";

PTA FAIR; *IT'S ALL IN THE FAMILY, McCALL'S*; JUNE 1964

It's *All in the Family* became a
smorgasbord of all the toys, games, fads,
and pastimes of a typical American family of
the fifties and sixties. There was everything
from hula hoops to horseshoes, drive-
in movies to driving ranges, little league
to lawnmowers, cub scouts, campfires,
Christmas, Thanksgiving, Halloween,
homework, swimming pools, basketball,
ballet classes, bowling, boxing, dance parties,
family reunions, babies, Monopoly, and
snow. There was even time left over to
clean out the attic.

"YEA-A-A-A, GRANDPOP! GRANDPOP! GRANDPOP!";

FAMILY REUNION; *IT'S ALL IN THE FAMILY*; *McCALL'S*; SEPTEMBER 1959

"Kinda takes you back, doesn't it?";

ATTIC; *IT'S ALL IN THE FAMILY*; McCALL'S; FEBRUARY 1964

DRIVE-IN THEATER; *IT'S ALL IN THE FAMILY*; *McCALL'S*; JUNE 1957

Return library books—stay for "Kiddies' Story Hour"; SATURDAY LIST; *IT'S ALL IN THE FAMILY; McCALL'S;* AUGUST 1958

"I made it, Mom! I'm a PEE-WEE!";

MINOR LEAGUER, UNPUBLISHED *IT'S ALL IN THE FAMILY* **SKETCH; 1964**

"Good morning, Ma'am, we are a group of boys—";

SUMMER WORK; *IT'S ALL IN THE FAMILY*; *McCALL'S*; AUGUST 1962

"Now, look, we've got a couple of weeks to go till Christmas . . . ";
ALL THROUGH THE HOUSE; *IT'S ALL IN THE FAMILY*, *McCALL'S*; DECEMBER 1959

"They're always after their daddy to do that, but—you know—by the time he gets home he's so tired.";
THANKSGIVING DAY; *IT'S ALL IN THE FAMILY*; *McCALL'S*; NOVEMBER 1956

"Now—all those in favor of a walk in the woods.";

CUB PACK; *IT'S ALL IN THE FAMILY; McCALL'S;* OCTOBER 1964

"Mr. Johnson says will you please come to the rear. He wants to talk to you about something.";

CUB PACK; *IT'S ALL IN THE FAMILY;* McCALL'S; OCTOBER 1964

"Freeze!"

CUB PACK; *IT'S ALL IN THE FAMILY*; *McCALL'S*; OCTOBER 1964

"Then a dry wind stirred the ashes on the hearth, and a voice from the chimney said, 'I am the ghost of Heathcliff Castle'";

CUB PACK; *IT'S ALL IN THE FAMILY;* McCALL'S; OCTOBER 1964

"But we haven't touched Juniper Street or Wellington Road, and there's that whole new development down by the park.";

TRICK OR TREAT; *IT'S ALL IN THE FAMILY;* **McCALL'S; OCTOBER 1957**

"And for the witch with the tallest hat.";

HALLOWEEN PARTY; *IT'S ALL IN THE FAMILY*; *McCALL'S*; OCTOBER 1959

"Neptune! What happened to Neptune?";

HOMEWORK; *IT'S ALL IN THE FAMILY*; *McCALL'S*; SEPTEMBER 1963

"Yeah. Coach Davis told us about that type of shot. He said is was quite popular during the earlier days of the game.";

BASKETBALL; *IT'S ALL IN THE FAMILY;* **McCALL'S; JANUARY 1963**

"Hi, Bill! Hi, Jim! Hi, Jane! Hi, Lee! Hi, Jill! Hi, Ted! Hi, Deb! Hi, Jack! Hi, Fred! Hi, Candy! Hi, Norm! Hi, Bob!..."; **SWIMMING POOL; *IT'S ALL IN THE FAMILY*; *McCALL'S*; JULY 1958**

"Come on in the house. Read your paper. Have a little supper. Then, later, when you can have it all to yourself . . . "; **SWIMMING POOL; *IT'S ALL IN THE FAMILY*; *McCALL'S*; JULY 1958**

"I just broke my record for consecutive pirouettes!";

BALLERINA; *IT'S ALL IN THE FAMILY; McCALL'S;* OCTOBER 1962

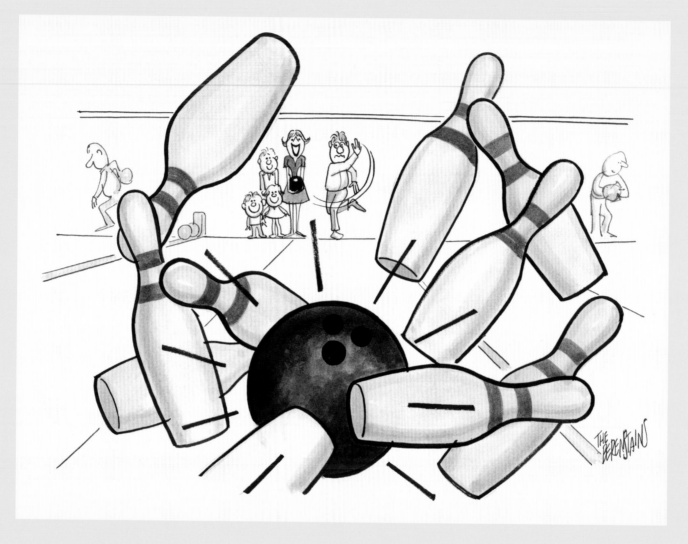

"Oh, I like that! Show us how to do that!";

BOWLING; *IT'S ALL IN THE FAMILY*; *McCALL'S*; APRIL 1962

"One little suggestion. Next time, after you throw the right—";

THE MANLY ART; *IT'S ALL IN THE FAMILY; McCALL'S;* **NOVEMBER 1962**

"Three . . . four . . . five . . . ";

THE MANLY ART; *IT'S ALL IN THE FAMILY; McCALL'S;* **NOVEMBER 1962**

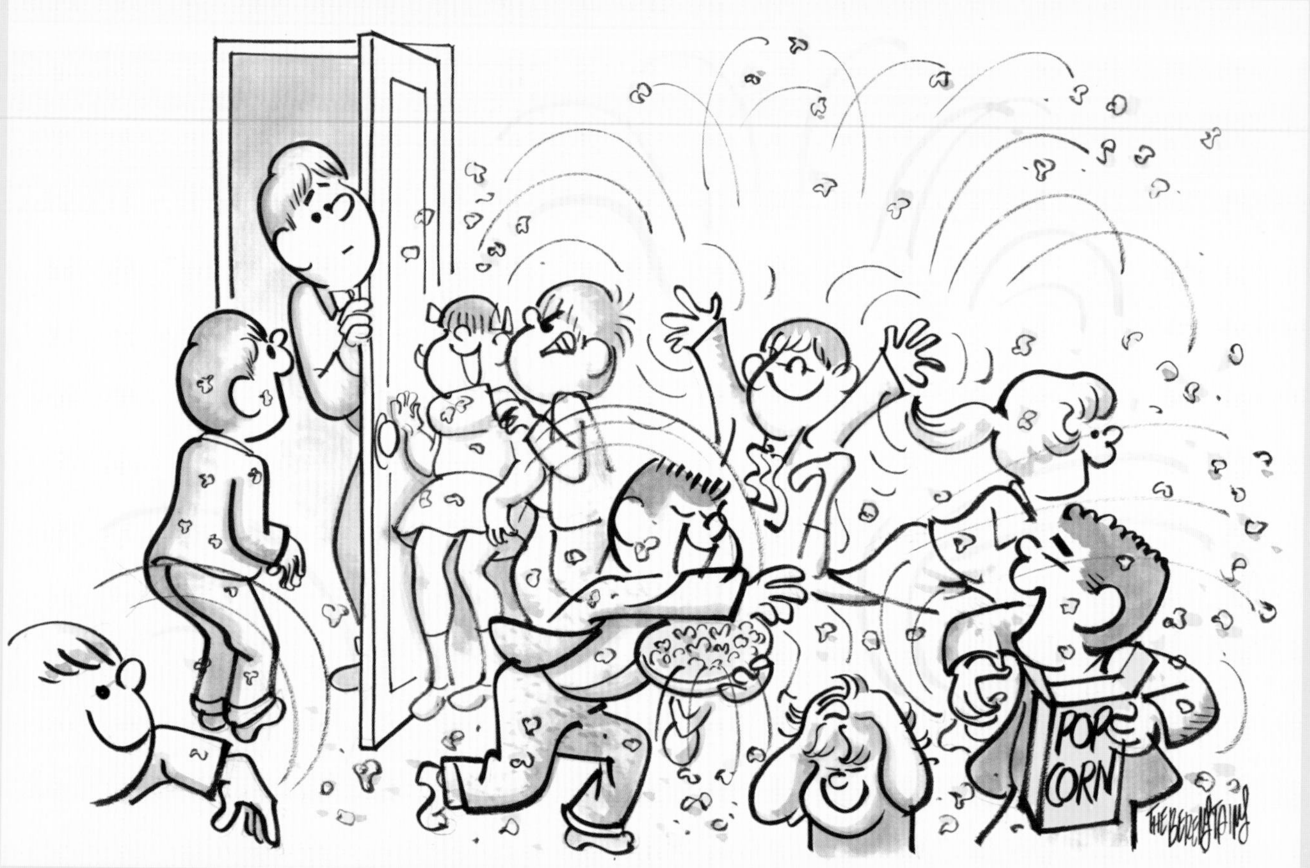
POP
CORN

"Did you want to see me about something, Dad?"

PARTY; *IT'S ALL IN THE FAMILY*; *McCALL'S*; NOVEMBER 1960

"We don't belong to any branch of the family. We live over on Gillespie Street.";

FAMILY REUNION; *IT'S ALL IN THE FAMILY*; **McCALL'S; SEPTEMBER 1959**

"Young lady, I have the greatest respect for Doctor Spock, both as a man and as a pediatrician. Nevrtheless—";

NEW BABY NEXT DOOR; *IT'S ALL IN THE FAMILY;* **McCALL'S; OCTOBER 1963**

"What shall we play now?";

FATHER'S DAY; *IT'S ALL IN THE FAMILY; McCALL'S;* JUNE 1959

"YIPPEE! IT'S STARTING AGAIN!";

SNOWY DAY; *IT'S ALL IN THE FAMILY;* **McCALL'S; FEBRUARY 1960**

"Hey, look! Here's my water rifle that I thought was lost . . . Hey! There's a whole lot of stuff here that I thought was lost!";

ATTIC; *IT'S ALL IN THE FAMILY*; *McCALL'S*; FEBRUARY 1964

A unique opportunity came Stan and Jan's way when, in addition to their regular cartoon feature, *McCall's* asked them to illustrate an article about childhood summer activities. It had the rousing title, "Fun Ideas for Little Children—101 Things to Do Outdoors and Indoors," and presented recipes for children's play using found objects—ordinary things from around the house and yard. This type of traditional, catch-as-catch-can children's playtime was already sinking beneath the great wave of 1950s' commercial toys when the piece was published.

Today, in the age of video games, I-pods, I-phones and I-don't-know-whats, the childhood world here depicted seems like something dug up by an archaeologist. Still, it gave my parents—and especially my mother who was responsible for the bulk of the art—a chance to create an absolutely charming evocation of childhood's summers past. The original captions from the article might have been dug up by an archaeologist, as well.

FUN IDEAS FOR LITTLE CHILDREN; *McCALL'S*, JULY, 1957

These children got two sheets to call their own, cut windows and doors.
Corner of a six-foot fence is two sides of playhouse.

Smocks are to wear while doing messy work.
Father's old shirts are good smocks. Mother's
blouses fit three-year-olds. A shirt or blouse
is a smock only after it has been put on
backwards and buttoned.

Paper Bag Party: Pack everyone's lunch in a paper bag and help the
children decide where a good place to eat—outside—would be. This
could also be called "camping" if you provide a few blankets and a
thermos of something. Children could come as cowboys, Indians,
pirates—or in any costume they own.

Wind bells: Use the lid of a coffee can. Punch
several holes around the sides; attach paper clips,
nails or any small hardware that will jingle in
motion. Hang it in an open window.

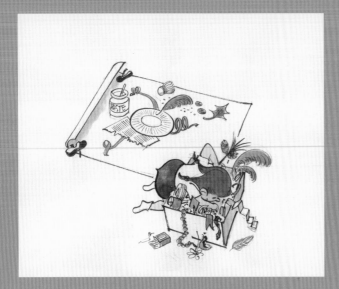

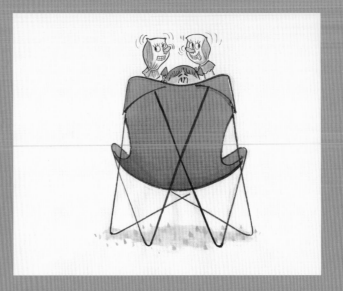

Collage: This is a technique especially suitable for small children. A child's interest is bound to hold when he is set before a collection of paper, metallic papers, paste, feathers, ribbons, excelsior, cellophane tape, soda straws, colored sequins, scraps of fabric. And he's sure to have an original picture worthy of framing.

Paper-bag puppet: Make a face on a small paper bag. Put bag over child's hand; secure with a rubber band around wrist

Musical washboard: Find as many thimbles as you can and let the child put them on her fingers and rub them across the bumps of the washboard. Popsicle sticks, wooden ice-cream spoons make good strummers.

She can help you prepare some of the things for lunch and dinner

When he wants you, he can ring a bell, blow a whistle or call through a megaphone.

a kaleidoscope, microscope or magnifying glass

Fringing burlap for placemats, coasters etc.

The sheer artistry of Stan and Jan's work is something often overlooked—naturally enough since they never made a point of technical display, preferring to use their skills to put their jokes across more effectively. Still, it comes strikingly into focus when the sketch versions of their cartoons are compared with the finished versions. Frequently, an entirely new layout and caption would evolve from the first sketch concept.

THE NEST; *IT'S ALL IN THE FAMILY*; *McCALL'S*; MAY 1963

"EGGS! EGGS! FOUR LITTLE BLUE EGGS!"

Sketch version

"EGGS IN THE NEST! EGGS IN THE NEST!"

Finished version

Some perfectly good gags never made
the final cut for publication and remained at
the sketch stage.

"Two more twigs and a piece of string!";

UNPUBLISHED SKETCH

"I know it's an awfully big favor but I wonder if you'd consider keeping your cat in for a day or two. . .";

UNPUBLISHED SKETCH

Here, too, can be noted the process of tweaking the caption. Often, the *McCall's* editors seem to have preferred cuter to funnier.

"Flying lessons."; **Sketch version**

"Three flying, and one to go."; **Finished version**

Sometimes a fluid spontaneity appears in the sketch, which is almost more appealing than the polish and detail of the finish. Some sketches depict the same scene from a different point of view, giving it a completely new feel.

Sketch version

Finished version

Unpublished sketch

Studying the entire sketch-to-finish process of one feature, Minor Leaguer, is illuminating. In some cases, the sketch and finish versions are virtually identical. But, frequently, major changes in layout, caption or basic concept occur. Also, more cartoon ideas were always submitted than could be used in the published feature. Occasionally, the rejects were the funniest of the batch.

MINOR LEAGUER; *IT'S ALL IN THE FAMILY;* **McCALL'S;**
MAY 1964

"Now look, you two, it's difficult enough being the youngest.";
Finished version

Title spot, sketch version

Title spot, finished version

"Boy, you've really got your work cut out for you, Mom."; **Sketch version**

"Help you, madam?"; **Finished version**

Sketch version

"Just smoke it in, Bill Baby! Just hit the old target!"; **Finished version**

O.K. BABY! JUST BURN IT IN, BILL BABY! JUST HIT THE OLD TARGET, BABY!..."; **sketch version**

"All ballplayers in this line! All mothers behind this fence!."; **Finished version**

Sketch version

"My youngest"; **Finished version**

Sketch version

"Oh, yes, Madam, the Mickey Mantle model is one of our finest numbers." **Unpublished sketch**

"Easy out, Junior! Stick it in his ear!" **Unpublished sketch**

The *It's All in the Family* features dealing with baseball are powerfully nostalgic for me, evoking the endless baseball-laden summer afternoons of the '50s and '60s. Though not much of a hand at the game myself, older brother, Leo, was totally baseball-obsessed. I can hear the smack of the ball in my father's catcher's mitt now, as Leo warmed up for a performance on the Little League pitching mound.

Even more meaningful for me, personally, are the cartoons devoted to a particular passion of mine growing up—one which I shared with my father—building model aircraft. We often sat up late into the night trying to finish a particularly challenging project. The feature, Model Father, presented here in the calligraphically rendered sketch version, perfectly captures that classic father-son experience. The assembly directions, so deftly employed as captions, also perfectly capture that incomprehensible technical double-speak so familiar to any long-suffering modeler.

MODEL FATHER; *IT'S ALL IN THE FAMILY*;

McCALL'S; **FEBRUARY 1958**

"Your Pegasus H-21 Helicopter Kit has been designed for the utmost authenticity and ease of construction. Familiarize yourself with the contents and proceed with easy step-by-step assembly."

"You will find in your kit a small sheet on which are various numbers, titles and insignia. This is your DECAL SHEET . . . "

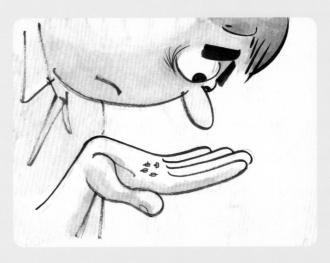

"Examine SPROCKET HUBS A, B, C, D. Cement UPPER SPROCKET HUB A in UPPER HUB SEAT. Cement LOWER SPROCKET HUB B in LOWER HUB SEAT. Cement LEFT SPROCKET HUB . . . "

Grasp the FUSELAGE in the left hand, pressing the thumb and forefinger against the CANOPY LOCK TABS. At the same time press COCKPIT CANOPY onto fuselage nose until it snaps into place . . .

"Grasp the FUSELAGE in the left hand, pressing the thumb and forefinger against the CANOPY LOCK TABS. At the same time press COCKPIT CANOPY onto fuselage nose until it snaps into place . . . "

"Don't rush. Proceed step by step in a calm, deliberate manner."

"If any part should need replacement, it may be ordered by number from Authento Plastics, Bismarck 3, North Dakota . . ."

"Your Pegasus H-21 Helicopter is now complete. Some other kits in which you may be interested are the X-66 Ram Jet Helicopter, the Sky Mule S-55 Windmill, the Dyno Twin Rotor . . . "

It's All in the Family migrated from *McCall's* to *Good Housekeeping* in the 1970s. I had the good fortune to work on the feature in its last few years under my parents' close (and strict) supervision. We finally decided to retire the feature in 1988.

Of course, by then, the hugely popular Berenstain Bears children's book series, which made its debut in 1962, had come to dominate the creative life of my parents and, later, myself. The transition from cartoons about children to books for children was a natural one for Stan and Jan. As parents themselves, they were interested and critical consumers of children's books.

Their professional interest was aroused, as well, when many former cartoonists came into prominence in the children's book field during the early sixties. Most prominent of all was Theodor Seuss Geisel, also editor and publisher of the new Random House Beginner Books line, an outgrowth of Geisel's groundbreaking early reader, *The Cat in the Hat*.

"I warned him not to look in the mirror.";

HALLOWEEN FEATURE, *IT'S ALL IN THE FAMILY, McCALL'S*; MID-1960s.

Stan and Jan decided to try their hands at the creation of a children's book and found the result good. When they submitted it to Dr. Seuss, he agreed with them. "Ted" became their first children's book editor as well as their chief exhorter, mentor, fan and, at times, slave-driver in their newly-chosen careers as children's authors and illustrators. They created about twenty books with Geisel, and then went on to produce about two hundred more over the next forty-odd years.

ATTA BABY!"; MINOR LEAGUER; UNPUBLISHED SKETCH; *IT'S ALL IN THE FAMILY*; 1964

"And we saw a real deer, and we cooked hot dogs on the end of a stick, and—";
CUB PACK; *IT'S ALL IN THE FAMILY*; McCALL'S; OCTOBER 1964